1,000,000 Books

are available to read at

Forgotten Books

www.ForgottenBooks.com

Read online
Download PDF
Purchase in print

ISBN 978-1-330-69819-8
PIBN 10093837

This book is a reproduction of an important historical work. Forgotten Books uses state-of-the-art technology to digitally reconstruct the work, preserving the original format whilst repairing imperfections present in the aged copy. In rare cases, an imperfection in the original, such as a blemish or missing page, may be replicated in our edition. We do, however, repair the vast majority of imperfections successfully; any imperfections that remain are intentionally left to preserve the state of such historical works.

Forgotten Books is a registered trademark of FB &c Ltd.
Copyright © 2018 FB &c Ltd.
FB &c Ltd, Dalton House, 60 Windsor Avenue, London, SW19 2RR.
Company number 08720141. Registered in England and Wales.

For support please visit www.forgottenbooks.com

1 MONTH OF FREE READING

at

www.ForgottenBooks.com

By purchasing this book you are eligible for one month membership to ForgottenBooks.com, giving you unlimited access to our entire collection of over 1,000,000 titles via our web site and mobile apps.

To claim your free month visit: www.forgottenbooks.com/free93837

* Offer is valid for 45 days from date of purchase. Terms and conditions apply.

English
Français
Deutsche
Italiano
Español
Português

www.forgottenbooks.com

Mythology Photography **Fiction**
Fishing Christianity **Art** Cooking
Essays Buddhism Freemasonry
Medicine **Biology** Music **Ancient Egypt** Evolution Carpentry Physics
Dance Geology **Mathematics** Fitness
Shakespeare **Folklore** Yoga Marketing
Confidence Immortality Biographies
Poetry **Psychology** Witchcraft
Electronics Chemistry History **Law**
Accounting **Philosophy** Anthropology
Alchemy Drama Quantum Mechanics
Atheism Sexual Health **Ancient History**
Entrepreneurship Languages Sport
Paleontology Needlework Islam
Metaphysics Investment Archaeology
Parenting Statistics Criminology
Motivational

TRAINING INFANTRY

BY
JOHN F. MORRISON
Colonel of Infantry

U. S. CAVALRY ASSOCIATION
Fort Leavenworth, Kansas
1914

COPYRIGHT, 1914, BY JOHN F. MORRISON

Ketcheson Printing Company
Leavenworth

PREFACE

In my commissioned service of over thirty-three years I have spent over twenty-two years with my regiment and three years in training a battalion of college cadets. I have been intimately associated with the national guard of one state and have had experience with the guard of four other states. I have seen something of foreign troops in both peace and war. In these many years I have observed the methods of training employed by a number of officers.

Our infantry training has improved over what I first knew but there still exists in places a lack of completeness and system. Of late years a much greater interest than formerly has been taken in the tactical instruction and training of our officers and the progress has been marked. The tactician is, however, but the skilled mechanic; the tools with which he works are his troops. New recruits are like the lump of ore, of no use until converted into steel and then forged into shape. The making of this tool from the raw material is our principal business during peace.

PREFACE

At the request of officers with whom I have often talked and corresponded on the subject of training infantry, this little book of suggestions has been prepared. It is based on my own experience and observation and what others have told me of their work. It is offered by an older officer to his younger brothers in the infantry in the hope that it may be of some service to them.

J. F. M.

CONTENTS

		PAGE
PREFACE		3
INTRODUCTION		7

CHAPTER		
I	THE ESSENTIAL AND THE DESIRABLE KNOWLEDGE AND HABIT	9
II	GENERAL DISTRIBUTION OF TIME WINTER AND SUMMER WORK	19
III	FIRE SUPERIORITY . . . FIRE DISTRIBUTION, CONTROL AND DISCIPLINE, SIGNALS	32
IV	COMBAT . . . . . THE COMPANY, BATTALION, REGIMENT	44
V	ARTILLERY FIRE . . . EFFECTIVENESS, FORMATIONS TO MEET TEAM PLAY	70
VI	PATROLS, ADVANCE AND REAR GUARDS, OUTPOSTS	89
VII	MARCHING . . . . . PREPARATIONS, INSTRUCTION, PRACTICE	104
VIII	THE NATIONAL GUARD . . . ESSENTIAL TRAINING FOR, ARMORY WORK AND SUMMER CAMPS	113

CONTENTS

- IX   INSPECTIONS 130
  YEARLY, COMPANY AND BATTALION EXAMINATIONS
- X   TRAINING A NEW REGIMENT . 134
  PRINCIPLES, SCHEDULE FOR
- XI   RECRUITING 161
  NEED FOR A CHANGE, PLAN, REASONS
- XII   IN CONCLUSION 177
  RELATIVE VALUES, STRENGTH OF THE COMPANY, OUR RESPONSIBILITY

INTRODUCTION

There is nothing more important to an army than the correct training of its infantry. The training of all the arms has much in common, but training infantry, owing to the manner of its use in battle, calls for much that is not required in the other arms.

Importance of training infantry

The infantry soldier must work more independently than men in the other branches. He cannot be led or controlled as can men in groups or close formations; hence he needs to be more thoroughly instructed in the part he is to play. This instruction cannot be given him on the field of battle. The man who must steadily advance on an enemy in position requires not only higher training but higher discipline than one who does his fighting in close formation, or at long range and out of sight of the enemy and protected from hostile fire by steel shields.

The mere mechanical part of the drill of all the arms is not difficult as regards its execution on the peaceful drillground but it requires much training to carry out these same things on the battlefield.

Importance of infantry training

It is reported as an incident in the recent Balkan War that a general of division, whose infantry had been reinforced by the addition of fifty per cent of recruits who had only received about a month's training, prepared for battle by sending all his new men to the rear, preferring to fight without them. His division was successful but the other divisions, which retained their new men in ranks during combat, broke and were routed.

War of today is not a game for amateurs. Infantry to be of any value has not only to be trained but to be properly and thoroughly trained. On the part of those in charge of this training there is necessary an appreciative understanding of the objects sought, earnest effort, tact, enthusiasm, and a real knowledge of men.

I

THE ESSENTIAL AND THE DESIRABLE KNOWLEDGE AND HABIT

TO ensure the proper training of our infantry there are needed competent officers—officers who know what should be taught and how to teach it. One sometimes hears: "He is a good practical soldier but he knows nothing of the theory." Such an expression is an absurdity. A man may know the theory yet be unable to apply it or make practical use of it; we have all seen such men. But a man cannot practice what he does not know. The knowledge of theory required by the junior commander is not great and the time it takes to learn it is short compared with the time required to master its practical application and to instruct properly a command. *(Practice and theory)*

The first requisite for a unit commander is a knowledge of the fundamental principles of the tactics of his arm and its employment in combination with the other arms, especially with the artillery. He must have a clear *(Needs of the unit commander)* conception of the modern battlefield in order to understand for what he must train his unit. He must train it for battle conditions, not peace conditions. A company trained to be handled exclusively by word of command, as in a close order drill on the parade ground, lacks the training that fits for battle.

Needs of the unit commander

The more the enlisted men know of the art of war the better. Time is not available however, to teach them the whole art of war even if the men in ranks were capable of mastering it. The instructor must therefore clearly understand what are the things the men *must* know and what are merely *desirable* as additions to their training. Every effort should be spent and all available time devoted to first perfecting the men in the things they *must* know; afterwards, if more time is available, it is well to extend in other directions their education and training.

Essential and desirable instruction

Under the first heading, *essentials*, the men must be taught their close order drill. This is necessary for two reasons: it renders possible the orderly movement of troops and it makes for discipline. So far as the orderly movement of troops is concerned very little is necessary but without precision close order drill is of no value towards discipline. To have a disciplinary value, drill movements must be carried out with exactitude. Discipline is injured if, when an officer gives a command at drill, it is only carried out approximately; the soldier is acquiring the habit of slighting his work and of doing an approximation, not the precise duty demanded of him. *Close order drill*

It takes but little longer to learn to execute correctly the few movements prescribed than to learn them incorrectly, but it requires constant attention on the part of the instructor to maintain exactness. The attention and effort required on the part of the instructor are, however, amply compensated by the results.

The men must know perfectly the mechanism of the extended order drill. A company must be able without confusion or mix-up to form line of skirmishers in the least possible time from any formation and facing in any direction. This will necessitate much practice. It does not take long to learn to form line of skirmishers quietly, from line or column of squads, facing to the front; but that is not sufficient. *Extended order drill*

The men must know how to estimate distances, how to shoot, how to use the bayonet;

Other essentials

they must understand patrolling and outpost duty, the construction of hasty intrenchments, the application of first aid, how to cook the ration and how to care for their arms and equipment.

Especially important is it that the men know how to march and how to care for themselves in the field. However well instructed a soldier may be he is of no use if at the time of battle he is back in the hospital.

Desirable instruction

Under the second heading, of things that it is desirable the men should know, are subjects which are essential for the officers to know but which are not equally essential for the men. Nevertheless it is an advantage to have them know as much as possible, provided the merely desirable instruction does not interfere with the proper training in essentials. Among these subjects are topography and the construction of temporary bridges; the list might be extended almost indefinitely.

Things to be understood and things to be made fixed habits

The instructor must further distinguish between the essential things which the men need merely to know or to understand and those which need to be practiced until they become habits. Those things the men will only be required to do off the battlefield,

KNOWLEDGE AND HABIT

where they will have time to think and be in condition to use their heads, need only be known.

Things to be understood and things to be made fixed habits

Psychology teaches us that under great stress of danger and excitement a man can be depended upon to do only those things which have become fixed habits, and further, that under these same trying conditions, a man who has acquired by practice a habit of doing something a certain way cannot do that thing differently. Action contrary to habit requires thought, and mental activity is difficult if not impossible under the circumstances. Acting according to habit is merely following the line of least resistance.

It is difficult to conceive of greater stress of danger and excitement than exists in a modern battle. Certainly there is no other case in which the knowledge of this psychological truth can be used to greater advantage than in training for battle.

As far as possible, then, all those things which the men must do under fire should be practiced until they become fixed habits. It has been said that if in the heat of battle a man even raises his rifle to his shoulder, before firing, it shows fair discipline. Not only must bringing the rifle to the shoulder be made

Fixed habits in battle

Habits of correct aiming and firing
a habit, but correct aiming and trigger pull whenever the rifle is brought to the shoulder must be made a habit, and one so strongly developed that these acts will always be done mechanically and without mental effort.

This desired result cannot be accomplished by two or three weeks a year of target practice. The training must be continuous for an extended period. To accomplish it altogether with ball cartridges would be too costly and often impracticable. The desired results can be obtained by pointing and aiming drills and gallery practice, if these are so conducted that the men never pull the trigger without properly bringing the rifle to the shoulder and looking through the sights at some target.

A week of continuous work every six months will not accomplish the results; frequent short drill periods are necessary. A man who starts in by smoking three strong cigars every Christmas and Fourth of July but not touching tobacco between times will not be so likely to acquire the smoking habit as one who starts very moderately and repeats the act daily. Overdoing any kind of training at one time, with long intervals between has a tendency to produce dislike rather than a habit. A few minutes of honest work at least twice every week, in pointing and aiming drill and gallery practice, will accomplish the result desired and my experience convinces me that it also produces much better results on the target range than crowding even more of this practice into the last month before going on the range. Certainly it is worth more than the other as a habit-former.

The better a man can shoot when the range is known to him the more important it is that his sight elevation be correct. A poor shot will scatter his bullets and may hit something even with a wrong elevation but the accurate shot will not hit anything; yet the correct range is valuable even to the poor shot.

<small>Estimating the range</small>

On the battlefield we can count only on our estimate of the range; seldom will it be practicable to determine it otherwise. Thus estimating distances has to be made a habit for two reasons: since habits alone count in battle, only by making it a habit can we depend on its being done; and second, it requires constant practice to enable men to estimate distances with fair accuracy.

Devoting two or three consecutive days

Estimating the range annually to estimating distances is almost a waste of time; practice should be had every week. I have seen both methods used and I am certain as to their relative values. How this instruction should be given will be mentioned later.

The deployments, advancing the attack, working by signals, taking advantage of cover, and in fact everything pertaining to combat from the opening of fire until the end of the battle must be practiced until it becomes a fixed habit on the part of the men.

The officer as instructor If we are to have good infantry the officers as instructors must be competent, have an appreciation of relative values, be able to distinguish between what is essential and what is merely desirable and make sure of essentials before spending time on the latter. Each officer must realize fully what has only to be known and what must be made fixed habit and govern his work accordingly.

Hints as to instruction work Now a few hints as to the instruction work. Never do this work in a perfunctory manner. Always have in mind what you want to teach and how you are going to do it. Put your heart in your work.

I have seen a well drilled company go to pieces under an officer who gave his commands in an indifferent manner and who gave too much "place rest." The spirit of indifference is contagious as well as the spirit of enthusiasm. If you have no keen interest simulate it and you will find it grow into the real thing. Remember that you are paid for good work and if you do not give this kind of service you are obtaining money fraudulently.

Hints as to instruction work

But not only have you yourself to keep interested; if the best results are to be obtained you must keep up the interest of your men. Nothing kills interest like monotony. There are so many things to be taught and there is so great an opportunity for variety that there is no excuse for not keeping the men interestedly busy for four hours a day.

Make clear to the men in the instruction work, particularly in the field training, not only the object sought but the why and wherefore. In maneuvers always explain the problem to them so far as is necessary to make them understand what the command is trying to do, where the enemy is supposed to be, and the rest. They will respond not only by taking more interest but by doing their part much better.

I have seen a flank patrol out at a maneuver the leader of which knew nothing of the supposed situation and had been given no instructions, except to act as left flank patrol. What interest could he be expected to take in the maneuver? How could he be counted on properly to perform his duty?

Callisthenic drill

I believe in carrying out this principle even in the callisthenic drill. Explain to the men the object of each movement, what muscle is to be developed by it and its advantage. Doing this makes this work much more profitable to the men as well as more interesting. It will also prevent our seeing these movements so executed as to deprive them of all their intended value.

Appeal to the intelligence of the men

In other words, treat the men being instructed as the intelligent men they are. They will both learn faster and do better work when they fully understand what is to be done and the reason why. A horse must be simply made to do certain things in a given way; it is a tedious process and a horse never does know much. Men trained as soldiers on the same plan as the horse give results out of all proportion to the time and effort spent. Why not, therefore, make use of the man's intelligence and simply help him train himself?

II

GENERAL DISTRIBUTION OF TIME

IN this country we cannot follow literally any of the systems of training adopted by the great military powers: our whole military system is too different. We can, however, profit by their experience and, if we translate, not the literal text of their regulations but the spirit, gain much. It is essential that any scheme of instruction adopted should be suited to our organization, method of recruitment and the various conditions surrounding our service.

The work must be so planned as to utilize all the available time of the year and in that time to cover all the absolute essentials of instruction. In this utilization of the time schools for non-commissioned officers and officers must be included. There is much ground to be covered during the year and unless the time be wisely apportioned it cannot be done. *Requisites of a system of training*

There is much of the work that can be done indoors; other work can only be done outside. Our troops are so widely scattered and under such varying climatic conditions that the distribution of time cannot profitably be the same for all.

Winter and summer work
Each post should make its own schedule. The work in each post must, however, be uniform. For example, in the northern part of the United States the year's training should begin November 1st and end October 31st. All the instruction that can be given during the winter months, should be given, leaving the rest for the open season. The schools for both officers and non-commissioned officers are held during the indoor season; the work done in them should dovetail in with the general scheme of instruction. Particular care should be exercised with respect to the **Schools** non-commissioned officers' schools; in them the non-commissioned officers should be taught thoroughly how to play their part in the varied work in the field and be given the reasons for things.

Simply repeating the words of a book should be avoided; teach them to do things. The company commander who is capable and in earnest can do much in winter toward training his company even in garrisons where weather conditions are the worst.

Most of the captains of one regiment known to me have been doing good work during the past two years in teaching the principles of the conduct of patrols and covering detachments. Some of them made use of the Stacey Relief Map; others simply built a sand table about ten feet by five. On this the sand was moulded to form hills and valleys. Blue strings were laid down for streams, yellow ones for roads. Minature bridges were constructed and placed where desired. Small twigs were used to make forests.

Methods of winter instruction

By means of practical examples worked out on these made or improvised maps the principles were thoroughly taught and more easily than is possible out of doors; when spring came, only a few exercises on the ground were necessary to make these companies proficient.

Another use made of the sand table was in the teaching of entrenching. Bull Durham tobacco sacks were converted into sand bags and the men taught their use in revetting, loop-holing, etc. Similarly on a minature scale were taught the preparation of head-logs, the making of gabions, facines and hurdle revetment. Brush work thus taught

Entrenching

indoors needs only be followed by one outdoor exercise, in which work is done on the scale actually used in the field, in order to render the company proficient.

Gymnasium

Where the post is so fortunate as to be provided with a gymnasium full advantage should be taken during the winter season of the opportunities for physical training which it affords. The physical development of the men is most important. Where no gymnasium is available a well-planned course in callisthenics is the best substitute and should be used. Callisthenics to music or for pure show should be prohibited.

First aid
Signalling

The indoor season must be fully utilized to save the full time of the outdoor season for that training which can only be given then. Instruction in such subjects as first aid and signalling naturally is given at this time. A place for gallery practice can always be rigged up.

Estimating distances

The foundation for estimating distances must be laid, and there should be practice in it every week, during the closed season. In this work the whole company should be employed together only for the first one or two exercises when the principles are being explained; after that a platoon or less at a time. Near each barracks there should be two stakes one hundred yards apart and so placed that the men see them every time the company forms. This is their unit of measure and cannot become too familiar to them.

<small>Estimating distances</small>

The captain or someone designated by him selects a couple of distances to be estimated. Each subdivision of the company then goes out in turn and upon completing the exercise returns and another goes out.

The men must be taught to estimate distances both from themselves to a given point and between two points, both at some distance from them. The latter is necessary in their patrol work in estimating lengths of column and frontages occupied. If the estimating be conducted in this way the weather will make little difference; the men dress suitably for it and are out only a short time. The work to be of value must be done under varying conditions of light.

There should be no week in the year in which this exercise is not conducted. In summer it should be done on the days when the company is away from the garrison on the weekly practice march; there is ample time for it during the long halt.

This work can be conducted so as only to

Estimating distances

take about fifteen minutes of each man's time per week. It is well worth it. I have seen the above plan carried out intelligently in two or three companies and the results were remarkably good; the ability of the men to estimate distance was better than that given for musketry school graduates in foreign services. On the other hand I have seen it indifferently carried out and, like most indifferent work, it was a waste of time.

Position and aiming drills, gallery practice

Position and aiming drills and gallery practice must be a weekly occurrence and holding them twice a week will be better. If the detachments are made small enough gallery practice requires but little time for each man. It is important in conducting this practice to see that no man ever fires a score in a careless or indifferent manner; if this is permitted the result obtained will be the opposite of that desired. I found one very effective means of preventing such careless work: a man found guilty of careless firing was required to repeat his score—but not at that time when it would delay the regular course. He had to remain near the gallery until I, or someone designated by me, came around to supervise his firing and it was usually some little time before I got around.

Throughout the year careful attention should be given to bayonet fencing. I do not believe that there is much probability of a bayonet contest in war but, for psychological reasons, this training is necessary. Positions are carried by the bayonet, but past experience shows that in such charges the bayonets seldom crossed and when they did it was a "rough and tumble." Our men may go in with the best intentions in the world to use the bayonet according to rule, yet the chances are that, in the excitement of the mêlée, habit will assert itself and the gun become a bat.

Bayonet fencing

Nevertheless, troops are very seldom "shot out of a position"; the imminent threat of the bayonet is necessary; but, as the opposing bayonets get close, one side or the other weakens.

It would be folly to expect men without bayonets to charge an enemy with long and sharp ones, or to expect them without bayonets to stand a charge by an enemy armed with such weapons, even though, if they had bayonets, they would be likely to club their rifles. The moral effect of a line of bayonets is great.

Kind of bayonet required

Infantry should be armed with the best of bayonets, long and, in war time, razor sharp. The men must have confidence in their ability to use them with skill and effect; otherwise they will neither charge nor stand the enemy's charge. At that stage of the fight success largely depends on the confidence of the individual man in his power to win.

Amount of bayonet practice Bayonet fencing should be continuous throughout the year. At least one-half-hour weekly should be devoted to it and during the indoor season extended and careful instruction should be given to groups not larger than a squad. During the outdoor season this instruction should be so arranged as not to interfere with the regular drills.

Division into sections for instruction The company should be divided into sections that can be handled conveniently for the instruction work. The success of the indoor work largely depends on keeping the sections small enough.

This is especially necessary in first aid and sandtable work. If the sections are too large at estimating distance and gallery practice it results in too much idle standing around.

Changing sections The sections must be changed from one class of work to another before the work drags or the men become tired of it. Give them variety.

The captain must exercise care in selecting the instructors for the various subjects. The man who will do it the best should be the instructor in each. Perfunctory or indifferent work should never be allowed on the part of an instructor or by the man being instructed. *Selecting instructors*

The capable, intelligent and honest captain will utilize the indoor season to the great benefit of his company and of his government. He will discover the best ways and means of instructing his own particular men. The incompetent captain, lacking average intelligence, will accomplish nothing under any circumstances. *The captain*

As much latitude as practicable should be given to subordinate commanders in carrying out any system of instruction and they should be held strictly responsible for results. A scheme in which there is laid down just how each thing is to be taught, and how much time and what time is to be devoted to it, is radically wrong. We need to develop our officers as well as our men. The conditions are different at different posts. The needs of different companies at the same posts are varied. Each captain should know just how much time he has and what is absolutely *Initiative in the instruction work* required of him in that time. He should then be allowed to work out his own solution of the problem.

Initiative in the instruction work

When every detail is prescribed the officer has no initiative, his interest is diminished, he thinks less, exercises less responsibility, and his work is not so good. If that policy be kept up long enough the subordinate officer will never do anything without positive instructions. An officer who exercises no judgment is of no value in war.

But absolute liberty for the subordinate to do as he pleases is impracticable. The regiment is a team of which his unit is only one member. There must be team play and every member must know and be able to do his part. The company must be taught certain things or it will not fit into the battalion team; the battalion must be fitted for the regimental team. Each larger unit must have time for training and has a right to demand that each lower unit which forms a part of it shall have accomplished its own special work on time and be ready to play its part in the work of the larger unit.

The regiment a team

The colonel is responsible for the training of his regiment. He should allot the time, supervise the work and see that every

The colonel

member of the team is ready. He is the best judge of the requirements of his regiment. But the colonel should do this so as to leave all the liberty practicable to subordinate commanders.

If all our captains were competent and reliable this work of the colonel would be very simple. But there are a few captains, unfortunately, who are far from the best, whose long suit at drill is "place rest" and having a sergeant drill the company in Butts' Manual. While more restrictions are necessary for such captains these restrictions do not hamper the others; they merely prohibit things the right kind of captain would never think of doing or require what he would never think of omitting. *Orders and restrictions*

Of course most of the instruction time belongs to the companies; it is in them that most of the work must be done. Four well trained companies under a competent major can be made into a well trained battalion in a very few days, and the time required for each higher unit is less than that for the one next below. *Time to organizations*

To the company belongs all the indoor season. In dividing the rest of the year for the northern part of the U. S. I believe that the available time from April 1st to October 1st should be allotted in the proportion of 4 days to the company for each 2 to the battalion and 1 to the regiment. The month of October should be devoted to maneuvers and to work in higher units. The time spent on the target range is excluded in computing the available time but no company should be allowed to devote more than two weeks to target practice exclusive of field firing; of the latter we can hardly get too much. It is appreciated that conditions at various posts make different schedules necessary.

<small>Time to target practice</small>

In the past we have seen the training done in a back-handed way: work in the higher units first, finally down to the company and soldier. This is so unlikely to occur in future that its evil results are not worth mentioning.

Too much time should not be devoted to close order drill, especially during the outdoor season. An hour a day for the first five or six drills and thereafter fifteen minutes a day is ample. There should always be, however, at least ten minutes a day of snappy, precise close order work; this together with the ceremonies will keep the companies up to the standard. Too much close order drill becomes monotonous; when that happens the

<small>Time to close order drill</small>

command fails to improve even if it does not deteriorate.

The drills during the indoor season should be two hours long; for the rest of the year not less than three and generally from four to six hours daily.

Length of drills

FIRE SUPERIORITY

WE are told that in battle we must have fire superiority to win; and fire control and direction are held as important. I doubt if these terms are fully understood by all. A hope to aid some of our younger officers to a better understanding of these terms, and of the vital importance of fire distribution, is the excuse for this chapter.

Fire effectiveness in battle

A line of men firing with the rifle, if not disturbed or endangered by the fire of an enemy, can do approximately target practice work. Now let a heavy fire be opened on them, one that is fairly accurate and well placed, and their work falls off very greatly; the heavier the fire they are subjected to the less effective becomes their own fire.

Careful study and research by competent men of foreign armies leads to the conclusion that if this line, when not under fire, could make 280 hits in a given time, subjected to a heavy, well placed fire its effectiveness would fall to $1/40$ or $1/70$; that is, from 280 hits to 7 or 4.

This looks extreme at first thought; but what captain with a good company but would know that he could deploy his company at from 800 to 1000 yards from a line of lying down figures and get a hit for at least every 10 shots. Yet history tells us that it takes from 1200 to 2000 shots in battle to put a man out of action. In the light of these facts our first figures look very moderate. *Fire effectiveness in battle*

With our present infantry arm an advance against a hostile line doing 280 work is impossible. Bring the enemy's effectiveness down to the four and keep it there and you can advance and win.

Fire superiority does not mean that you are firing more shots than the enemy, it does not mean he is firing less than you; it means that your fire has become so close and effective that he has lost his nerve and is shooting wildly.

To obtain this fire superiority certain things are necessary. We must have proper fire distribution. To explain this let us assume that a hostile line is 200 yards long, that our force is the stronger. We concentrate our fire on the right half of the hostile line, leaving the other half untouched. The effectiveness of the fire of half of this line re- *Fire distribution*

Fire distribution

mains at 280, the other half falls to 2, average 141; our advance is impossible. We now cover the entire target and its fire effectiveness falls to 7; our advance is possible.

Fire superiority is possible, then, only if we have fire distribution. It is not sufficient to fire a certain number of shots at part of the line, the whole hostile line must be subjected to a nerve racking fire to reduce the effectiveness of its fire.

Another thing to be considered is that the enemy will conceal himself as much as possible. On a large part of the hostile line no one will be seen; men will be hidden by tufts of grass, bushes, etc. But while this cover conceals the enemy from our view, he sees our location and his fire is not interrupted. There is a strong tendency to shoot only at the men that can be seen. This must be overcome; much of our firing must be aimed at a locality, although unseen the enemy is nevertheless there and his fire effectiveness must be kept down. Our fire must be distributed to cover every part of the hostile line whether the enemy is seen or not.

To secure this fire distribution we must be able to direct the fire of our men, to place it where wanted. But direction necessarily implies control; you can not direct what you cannot control. Thus a fire control system which will work on the battlefield is a primary requisite to success.

Fire control

Another term used is fire discipline. The word fire adds nothing to its meaning; but discipline is vital to success. No matter what your system of control, if the men do not respond with prompt obedience it is worthless. Disciplined men can be counted on to do what is wanted if they know how, others cannot. There is no fire discipline distinct from other military discipline.

Fire discipline

To sum up: fire superiority is necessary to success, to attain fire superiority we must properly distribute our fire, to do this we must be able to control and hence direct it, and this can only be done if our men are disciplined. An attack with raw troops is possible only against still poorer ones.

Our fire control and direction needs more explanation. A method must be had which will work on the battlefield. No one who has seen a modern battle will think for a moment that it is practicable to control and direct a firing line by verbal orders. A battalion commander must be far enough to the rear

Method of fire control

to observe his entire line. In the noise of a real battle his voice could not be heard ten yards by men on the firing line. The same is equally true of company and platoon commanders. These officers cannot be running up and down the line giving instructions; if they tried it they would not last long.

Use of signals

Our method must therefore be one that can be executed independently of the voice and with as little exposure of the officers as practicable. The method by signals given in our I. D. R. answers the requirements. The text of it can be learned in a few minutes, but to train a battalion so that it will fully respond under danger requires hours of practice: it is one thing that must become a habit.

After the mechanism of the drill is learned officers should conduct their line as in battle by signals only. Do not teach men to expect you to be running up and down the line personally correcting errors and giving directions, leading them to expect this to be done in battle. The effect of a decided change in conduct when danger is present is apt not to be good. Moreover, the command will not respond to signals alone on the battlefield if, in instruction work, they have never been taught to depend on them exclusively. We should do everything at battle exercises just as nearly as possible as it will be done in battle. *Use of signals*

I have seen at battle exercises men stand up in the open and wave their flags to give the signals. This is absurd. In battle it would be needlessly dangerous, would give the enemy too much information, and it is unnecessary. The necessary signals in the battalion can be given by a man lying on the ground with a handkerchief, or flag without the staff, and be seen for the short distances separating the major from his captains or the captain from his platoon commanders. Practice alone is required to enable this to be done efficiently. It must be so done in battle and must therefore be drilled that way.

It should be remembered that the new semaphore code recently adopted does not apply to these signals. The new code requires men to stand; the old must be used for these battle signals.

Additional signals to those given in the I. D. R. may be taught and used in companies. It is doubtful if they are necessary and if not necessary they are wrong. The more signals you have, the more chance of mistakes. *Additional signals*

Additional signals
Signals for forming squad or platoon columns are unnecessary. These movements are not executed close to the enemy nor when your line is firing, hence verbal commands are practicable and when practicable are desirable, are surer and easier.

Signals are necessary when your line has commenced the fire fight but from there on few commands are necessary; there are so few things that can be ordered, the time for maneuver and instruction is past. One or two of those given might be dispensed with and one for fixing bayonets should be added; possibly there are one or two others that should be added.

Observing fire effectiveness
We have discussed how to obtain fire superiority; how may we know when we have it, if the volume of the enemy's fire remains practically the same? Company and platoon commanders must watch for the effect of the enemy's fire, where his bullets are striking. If the hostile bullets are going wild, some striking far short, others way high, and very few are effective, you have fire superiority; that is the time to gain distance to the front. On the other hand, although you may be suffering no loss, you see that the enemy's bullets, well massed,

are striking, say 50 yards in your front; you have no fire superiority; the enemy has simply underestimated the range and your advance will bring you into the center of his beaten zone. But this is your opportunity to gain fire superiority. Your men are suffering little or no loss, should be less affected and should do better work. If this opportunity is well utilized you will gain fire superiority. *Observing fire effectiveness*

When you have fire superiority you must push the advance, take full advantage of your opportunity; if you temporarily lose it, suspend the advance until you regain the necessary superiority.

Fire properly distributed is one essential to gaining fire superiority. Proper distribution means it is placed *on* the target and on all of the target, not just one part. Placing our fire on the target requires that our men be at least fair shots, have their nerve and know the range. To cover all the target rather than concentrate on a part is not easy and to attain practical efficiency in this requires skill and practice. *Distribution of fire*

In the deployment for battle the division is generally given a specific mission, the division commander assigns to each brigade its part of the task, and so on down to the battalion, company, platoon and even squad.

Distribution of fire

There is little involved in the larger units except the tactical skill to know how to use the larger units to gain the required end; dividing the terrain is easy. It is difficult with the commanders of the smaller units; the division of the target generally becomes harder the smaller the subdivision. The major must divide his target, say between two companies, and do it so that there can be no mistake on the part of the captains as to just what part each is to cover. The company commander must then divide his section among his platoons and the latter often among the squads.

The captain's problems

The battalion commander has only one difficulty—to find a way to make each captain clearly understand where is the division of target and where its extreme limit. The company commander has a shorter line to divide and has to divide it into more parts. Landmarks are not so common as he will then desire.

The captain has another problem in this connection: shall he divide his target into four parts and assign each platoon a separate part, or into two parts and give two platoons the same target, i. e., 1st and 3d the right half, 2d and 4th the left half? The captain has not only the problem of finding proper dividing points in the target, but he must divide and allot the target so as to get the best fire effect. It might happen, as I once saw in a field firing problem, that the right platoon could not see the corresponding part of the target, hence was given the other extreme flank and the rest of the target divided accordingly. It is not the division alone, but what is the best division and allotment, that must be considered. *The captain's problems*

This will all be more clearly understood if you will go in the country and assume a regiment is ordered to attack a certain line under certain conditions, and then give the colonel's attack order, from that take each major's target and divided it between the companies and then divide each company target. This should, of course, always be done at the same distance from the target that you would have to make the distribution if a real enemy were there. You should have two or three men with you to act as the subordinates in each case and to determine whether the division is fully and perfectly understood. It is easy on a map, but often very difficult on the ground; distinctive marks are sometimes very scarce. *Practice in distributing the target*

Practice in distributing the target

Each commander should practice this, devising a method for himself that will work. Officers alone or together in small groups should practice it as a sort of tactical walk. But primarily it should be done in each unit: the colonel should take the majors on such a tactical walk; the majors their captains; the captains their platoon commanders. Estimating distance should be worked in the same exercise.

For the companies this is good work for the indoor season. There are days when work can be planned for the company that does not require the presence of the captain or of most of his officers and non-commissioned officers; these can then utilize the drill period as above described. It may be made a real tactical walk with special stress laid on the division and allotment of the target.

Assistance of artillery

It must be borne in mind that in most cases the artillery will play a large part in the gaining and maintaining of fire superiority. But this fact does not alter the work of the infantry; we must still do most of the killing and unnerving of the enemy and this is true whether the enemy consists of infantry alone or of infantry in conjunction with artillery.

In this chapter the first part is much like

"right line strategy" mathematics applied to a battlefield where little is subject to such treatment. But that seemed the easiest and simplest way to make clear to beginners terms that must be fully understood. It is hoped that that part of the chapter will be understood as meant, as offering merely a means of illustration and not as implying that a battle can be worked out with mathematical precision.

IV

COMBAT

WAR, according to Clausewitz, is the continuation of diplomacy. Diplomacy is not always able to settle international disputes, then the army must do what the diplomats have failed to accomplish. In our own history it has been the mass of the people who have forced our wars, and who, in the case of a strong public sentiment arising, will involve us again. On account of the state of preparedness of most great nations and because of the enormous cost of modern war, wars are shorter than formerly.

Object of an army
If this country becomes involved in a war with a military power it will be impracticable to learn the art of war and train an army after the outbreak; the war will not last long enough. The object of having an army is for war not for peace, and the battles alone really decide the issue; the battles are not numerous but each tends one way or the other to end the struggle. Great armies exist for many years between wars and are then trained for these few days of

battles which determine the fate of the nation. The whole aim of an army should be to be ready for war and the success or failure in war is determined by a few days of battle. Untrained troops are of no value on the modern battlefield.

Part of our close order drill, the ceremonies and some other things we teach, are accessories and, if given their proper place, are of value, but the battlefield is the crucial test; by our fitness for that must our training be judged. The work of generals and the general staff is vitally important but the best plan will accomplish nothing if there are no trained companies to carry out their part. Training for battle

In this chapter is considered the training necessary for combat. This is the work executed under the severest strain and under the greatest difficulties of leadership and control. This training must be thorough and the things in combat which have to be done must become a habit.

THE COMPANY

The first essential is that the men must know the mechanism of the extended order drill, including all signals used. To keep control of the skirmish line in battle, that is to Extended order practice

Extended order practice

maintain such order therein that it can be directed and used as desired, is far from easy. Excitement and confusion, especially in the last stages of the combat, are apt to occur. Everything possible must be done to preserve organization and control.

Much depends upon the start; if there is confusion at the start and the squads get mixed, success is more than doubtful. In the majority of cases the deployment will be made quietly at long range, but not in all. The company must be drilled until able to deploy from all formations, facing in any direction, in the least time practicable, and without any confusion or mix-up.

Calmness in giving orders

The captain who can give all his orders and commands at the start of a fight in a calm, unexcited manner has a great advantage over the one whose voice or manner indicates excitement. This calm manner should be cultivated during training. As good a way as I know for such training is to have a few men to represent hostile forces conceal themselves at various points in a moderately close country; march the company through this terrain and, as the represented enemy appears, form skirmish line facing the supposed enemy, give the range and the commands for opening fire in the least possible time. The captain himself should not know where the represented enemy will appear. This is training for the captain and also excellent practice for the company.

Occasionally during an advance points are reached where a company is sheltered from fire. Advantage should always be taken of such opportunities to reëstablish perfect order, replace fallen leaders and thus get a new start. Such an opportunity decidedly increases your chance of success in battle; real control is reëstablished. Practice this in your battle training when the opportunity offers, but never do it when, in a real combat, it would be impracticable. *Restoring order*

After the mechanism of the extended order drill is understood all combat exercises should have a problem or situation. These should always be simple; elaborate tactical problems for this instruction work are unnecessary. For a simulated attack as part of a line, all that is necessary is a statement that the enemy, a regiment of infantry, is holding the line from ——— to ———, our regiment is to attack it at once, our battalion on the right, we are the right company, our target or objective the part of the line from ——— to *Combat exercises*

———. This of course should be varied but need be no more complicated. The captain should give this to his whole company, let all the men know what they are supposed to be doing.

Situation and orders

The captain should then give his attack order, always carefully distributing the target. For a company operating alone the following form will answer every purpose: This company belongs to a division engaged with a hostile division five miles north of here. This company was detached to capture that building (pointing) which is assumed to be important. The defending force occupies the line ———. The order for the attack then follows. Usually in such a case, a small support would be held out. Of course the problems will vary according to what it is desired to teach. Always distribute the target and let the men understand what you are trying to do. All combat exercises should be

Method of conducting exercises

conducted as nearly as possible as though the enemy were real. Allow nothing to be done that would not be attempted were it real war, otherwise you do not give instruction but misinformation. After the mechanism is taught, the captain and platoon commanders must conduct themselves in combat exercises as they would under hostile fire, keep close to the ground, use signals only. After the exercise is over have a critique, point out the errors made and tell the command how they should be corrected. **Method of conducting exercises**

You must expect that if mistakes are made at the drill they will be made in battle; to correct these mistakes you should use only those means at drill that will be practicable in battle. The captain needs much practice in thus handling a skirmish line and those under him need more practice before the company can be well handled in this manner.

The effectiveness of the enemy's fire should be indicated that platoon commanders can practice the control of rushes. The simplest way to do this that I have found is to have a man at the hostile position with two little flags. Holding both of these vertically over his head means the enemy's fire is wild and nearly harmless. One flag vertical the other horizontal indicates a moderately effective fire. Both flags horizontal indicates the maximum effectiveness—that the enemy has a decided fire superiority. When both flags touch the ground it indicates no fire. **Means of representing enemy's fire**

The advance of the attacking force is only practicable by taking advantage of the times

Means of representing enemy's fire

when the fire is ineffective or weak to push forward, and, when the hostile fire is too strong, shooting to gain fire superiority. Platoon commanders and men must become accustomed to seizing these opportunities to advance and suddenly getting down when there is a burst of effective fire. The flags on the hostile position may be controlled by an instructor, stationed behind the company officers, indicating how the flags are to be held.

Remember that the hostile fire becomes more effective in proportion as ours is less effective. If we have the most men we should gain fire superiority if our shots are well placed. If the firing line has not distributed its fire properly the instructor causes both flags to be held horizontally; no advance is then possible until the company officers find out the cause of the trouble and correct it. The same is done whenever a serious error in sight elevation is made. Majors should frequently conduct such exercises with their companies. The company officers must become quick in determining why the hostile fire is more effective than suits existing conditions and learn to correct the error.

You may not be able to reduce the effectiveness of the hostile fire so that an advance under it is practicable and, in some cases, it may not be your mission to do so; but in every case where the hostile fire passes a certain point of effectiveness, depending on relative numbers, your range, distribution or something is wrong, or else your men have lost their nerve. Judging the effect of the hostile fire is something in which company and platoon commanders must be proficient, but off the battlefield this can only be taught in theory. *Judging defects in firing*

In advancing the attack by rushes the size of the fraction rushing will be dependent upon the relative proportion of rifles necessary to hold your fire superiority. If rushes are practicable at all it will seldom be necessary to rush by smaller units than the platoon. But an advance will sometimes have to be made by fractions of only a man or two and sometimes by crawling. All these should be taught. *Advance by rushes.*

When the enemy is active the rushes should not be long, if of only 25 or 30 yards the time the men are actually running will be very short, too short for the average man to pick up the target, raise the rifle to his shoulder and fire with careful aim. Too much time is taken by the average man in getting up and down. The men must be practiced in springing to their feet and getting down again in the shortest time possible. There is a knack in this not difficult to acquire.

Reinforcements
Reinforcing a firing line will generally bring about intermingling of squads and platoons. To avoid this by closing in on the center by companies, thus creating gaps for reinforcements, is impracticable on a battlefield when reinforcing is necessary. In battle in the great majority of cases reinforcements will go in as they can and fall into the existing gaps where found. As this will be the rule in battle we should so drill it.

When the next rush is made, say by squads, where do these reinforcements go? In one regiment at least, they solved it satisfactorily. The points of division along the firing line remain where they were; the new man who joins the firing line always goes with the man on his right, he belongs to the squad and to the platoon of the man on his right. This provision should be added in the I. D. R.

In teaching the mechanism of the extended order, practice should be had in this by dividing the company into firing line and support and then feeding in the support and continuing the advance by rushes. If you expect this to be done in battle it must become a habit. To get the best practice in this mixing, as well as to train officers and sergeants to think quickly and to act properly, there should be many rencontre engagements so planned as to bring about a mixing of units on the firing line. *Mixing on the firing line*

Some practice should be afforded with companies at war strength. This can be had by combining two or more companies. By this means it is sought to accustom officers to the fronts and depths of such a company and also to the greater length of time required to change formation. *Practice at war strength*

In combat exercises of the company alone practice must be had in shifting part of the fire to new targets and redistributing the old. In large battles this will seldom if ever be required by men in the firing line, but it will occur in detachment work. The companies should get practice in this and it can be well coupled with the instruction in hasty deployments suggested on page 46. *Redistributing the target*

Some work should be done on the defensive. A few men should be detailed to

Work on the defensive

represent the enemy; if the man carries one little flag he represents a squad, if two flags a platoon. These men should be in charge of a competent man who as nearly as is practicable directs their advance as such units would really advance under the assumed conditions. Enveloping movements and surprise attacks can thus be well simulated, giving the company the opportunity to practice meeting such movements by the use of the support, redistribution of targets, etc.

Company against company

The instruction against an outlined enemy having been practiced until the companies are well instructed, the enemy should be represented, one company should work against another. This gives an opportunity for reconnaissance work before and during the attack and introduces the elements of uncertainty as to what the enemy will do.

Night operations

In war, night operations are inevitable and we must recognize this fact and prepare for them. Night marches by large commands, patrolling by both large and small groups, and outpost work, including the establishing of the outpost in the dark, will all occur as well as an occasional night battle. In all this work the principal **difficulty** seems to be to avoid confusion **and** mistakes.

The men, especially those who are city bred, are unable to orient themselves in the dark. The darkness when coupled with possible unseen foes has a demoralizing effect and this effect will be the greater the more helpless the man feels himself to be in the dark and the less confidence he has in the ability of the company to act as a company. Much of this difficulty can be overcome by a little careful training. *Orientation*

The men should be taken out and taught to orient themselves by the stars and prominent features that can be distinguished at night. The effects of different backgrounds on the visibility of objects should be demonstrated, and especially the prominence of objects on a skyline. Estimating distance by sound should be practiced. The men grouped into small patrols should be made to find their way from place to place and then to operate against other patrols.

The company should be drilled at night. Forming line from column, front into line, on right or left into line, and even forming line of skirmishers, should be practiced and an occasional night march made. A very few drills each season, held at night instead of in daylight, will do much toward giving the men *Night drill*

Night drill

that necessary confidence in the ability of the company to work together in the dark.

It will sometimes happen that a command will have to go into camp after dark and establish an outpost. This should be practiced at least once each season after the company has been well instructed in the work by daylight.

Night attacks

Satisfactory training for night attacks is difficult. The first principle governing night attacks is not to shoot but to get in as close as possible undiscovered and then rush with the bayonet. It is impracticable to practice this with a represented enemy; it is too dangerous. To practice it by allowing the opposing sides to fire blanks at each other is all wrong because it is teaching the men to do what they should not do in war.

One method is to place men to represent the enemy behind a suitable fence, then to make the advance and attack, causing the represented enemy to open fire as soon as the attack is discovered. An open wire fence will not prevent the discovery of the attack but will stop the bayonet rush before anyone is hurt. This is not very satisfactory work for the company but is more appropriate for the battalion and regiment. In these latter it is desirable to practice the necessary formations for such attacks and to give the officers experience in such troop leading. For this work to be of benefit the officers must know their night tactics, the proper formations to take and the best methods of troop leading; this knowledge should first be acquired by study and then put to the test at night. It is not well to devote too much time to such work. **Night attacks**

In many posts practice can be had in tactical work in the woods. This opportunity should not be neglected. A good tactician will try to avoid a thick forest as a battlefield but with long lines of battle parts of the line will inevitably extend through forests. Hence the officers must study the principles governing woods fighting and seek to train the men so that they can play their part. Woods combat has many of the difficulties of night work. **Woods fighting**

There should be considerable work on fire problems; it is excellent practice, especially for the officers and non-commissioned officers. Field firing is not here meant but simulated firing. A simple problem is given and the officer or sergeant with a platoon or company solves it practically. By using a **Fire problem** few men with flags to represent the enemy and with a proper critique afterwards for all the company, great benefit should be derived.

Fire problems

As an example of such a problem: dispose one platoon of the company under cover near a ridge with a concealed man watching to the front and stationed about 25 yards from the platoon, the remainder of the company 400 yards in rear but in sight of the platoon. The following situation is then given out:

Fire problem against cavalry

"This company has been detached from a larger force back at X. Hostile cavalry is in this neighborhood and is doing much damage. The orders received when this company was detached stated that other companies were to go out on other roads and this company on this one to inflict as much punishment as practicable on this cavalry if encountered. We have reached this point and just halted for a ten minutes rest."

As soon as the situation is fully understood and the men are in their respective positions, a troop of cavalry, represented by a few men with yellow flags, comes in view of the sentinel and halts. Either verbally, or by a signal agreed upon, the captain explains that they have dismounted for rest. The sentinel and platoon commander now have their problem.

As another example take the same general situation in such terrain that a glimpse is caught of the troop moving along a road but immediately it passes behind cover; several hundred yards beyond, if it continues on the road, the troop will again come into view and be exposed for a considerable stretch of road and within rifle range. What is done now?

Fire problem against cavalry

After the exercise the captain assembles the company and criticises the errors made and points out what should have been done. In the first situation opening fire by a few men would result in the hostile troop's mounting and getting away with little damage or else in their getting their horses back under cover and being prepared to fight on foot. After the company once opens fire it will have a target but for a very short time; hence great care must be exercised in estimating the distance, dividing the target and giving the other necessary orders so as to produce the greatest effect in the least time. The captain should carefully study his problem and be prepared to give an instructive critique.

A little book called "Fire Problems" by T. D. Pilcher of the British Army is recommended to our officers; it treats this subject more fully, gives several problems and shows how the solutions should be criticized.

Suggestions for fire problems

Suggestions for fire problems

The problems must be gotten up, as a matter of course, to fit the ground you have. A great variety of fire problems is afforded by any terrain. There should be some problems in which more than one target is offered. In getting up problems do not let yourself be hampered by the critics who will tell you that a troop of cavalry would not have crossed your front without having discovered you or without having been warned by its patrols: you are teaching fire tactics, not cavalry tactics, and besides, even cavalry has been known to do foolish and careless things. Try to make the problem reasonable and one which might occur in war but do not discard a good fire problem which teaches a valuable lesson because the situation is one which ought never to arise in battle. Few problems that are tried out in maneuvers will ever be duplicated in that exact form in war but the tactical principles involved will recur often.

Distribution of fire problem

There is one field firing problem which, if practiced once each year, would do a world of good in securing fire distribution. A line of prone figures is placed to represent the enemy on ground so selected that, while the figures cannot all be seen by the attackers, yet a man in the place of each figure could see the ground over which the advance is made. The defensive line should not be straight; it would seldom be so in war, it must conform to the ground. There should be stretches of thirty or forty figures that are concealed, then groups in plain view; brush, clumps of heavy grass afford the kind of cover desired. Have the battalion go through the form of attacking this line, using ball cartridges. Then have the men inspect the targets, see how plainly they could have been seen by the enemy while the latter was out of sight and see the effect of cover on the fire drawn and the faults in distribution. After this carefully explain the results of a lack of distribution; point out that the long stretches of the hostile line not under fire would have been doing target practice work on your advancing line and what the resulting losses would have been.

Distribution of fire proble

It is an effective way of impressing on men's minds the necessity of proper distribution and of firing where directed whether they see anything or not. It also shows the advantage of cover, if only from view. The men must be taught to take advantage of cover, if only from view, whenever offered, if it can be done without interfering with their doing their work.

Combat against cavalry
For combat against cavalry the men must be taught in their bayonet work the proper way to oppose a man on horseback. How to meet a charge with fire must be largely theorectical but it should be carefully explained and, if a few mounted men are available to outline a charging force, some practical work can be had; it is a fire problem.

Special company problems
There are many problems in minor tactics that should form part of every company's training, such as forcing a defile or a bridge, passing through a village as a patrol or as advance party of an advance guard, passing a woods under the same conditions and, on the side of the defense, preventing a hostile force from doing these things. There may be no gorge or pass through hills in your immediate vicinity but the practice can still be had: two large buildings near together will answer for a defile; the garrison is a village. If there be no bridge, with a little imagination you can improvise something to answer. In this class of problems the captain must know the tactics of his problem and be able to explain it thoroughly. Generally in these problems detachments having important missions have to be made; give their commanders muc latitude in carrying them out and in your

critique point out the errors and how the work should have been done. It is well in all such problems to precede them by a simple talk to the whole company explaining the tactical principles governing the work. These problems can be made the most interesting part of the company's training.   *Special company problems*

Instruction must be given the company in meeting artillery fire and in the work of the various covering detachments but these two subjects, owing to their importance and length, are reserved for consideration in separate chapters.

The company commander must get the full help and support of his platoon and squad leaders, much depends upon them; they are the real leaders of the men; they require much training and practice, especially in leading the rushes and in controlling and directing fire.   *Hints for company work*

The discipline must be strict in these exercises, the men must never be allowed to slight the work. A certain amount of latitude must be given but prompt obedience to an order must be insisted upon. Without such discipline an attack is hopeless; the drill field is the place to acquire it.

In all this work keep the interest of the men. Occasionally take them to a shady

Hints for company work place and instruct them orally, explain the objects sought and the reasons for doing things in anything that is part of their proper training.

Do not keep at one class of work until the men are tired of it; vary the work. You can keep a company interested for four hours a day if you will only vary the instruction and put some soul into it. Give very little place rest; for a rest change the work. Combat exercises must be frequent. They are entitled to a large share of the time; the work of the firing line must be a habit.

THE BATTALION

Hints for battalion training The period of company training having been completed that of the battalion commences. The same general plan should be followed as in the case of the company. The mechanism of extended order should first be thoroughly learned, then the attack against an outlined enemy, then battalion against battalion. The enlisted men have little new to learn, the work for them is merely practice in what they have learned in the company training. For the captains it is instruction in team work and in tactics.

The battalion is the attack unit and as a

tactical unit is most important. An infantry attack is largely a combination of battalion attacks. Every exercise should be a problem which teaches some lesson as well as affords practice. The employment of combat patrols of some size can be made a part of the exercise and their proper use and leading taught. The use of the local support, how it is handled and how maneuvered, is a very important part.

<small>Hints for battalion training</small>

In these exercises the major must control his battalion as in battle. The absurdity of his riding around and giving verbal instructions to his firing line must not be permitted. A great part of the value of these combat exercises lies in the practice given in handling a battalion with the limited means of control possible on the field of battle and accustoming company commanders to carrying out their part under the same conditions. Majors thus learn to give their initial orders so as to insure the carrying out of their plan of action.

The battalion being the attack unit, whether alone or as part of a long line, its rushes are independent of those of other battalions although as a whole it keeps the general line. Each company of course must govern its advance by that of the others in

Hints for battalion training

the same battalion. An advance can only start from one flank or the other of the battalion and then continue successively to completion. Rushes never start from both flanks or the center; the reason for this is obvious.

The little flags mentioned under company training can be used in battalion training to even better advantage. Captains are more on their own responsibility in a battalion than are platoon commanders in a company and must act according to assumed existing conditions. In the battalion the shifting of fire from one target to another is less frequent than in the company. New unexpected targets are cared for, as a rule, by the support.

Battalion commanders have more need of reconnaissance and must get experience in ordering it properly and judging the reports and basing their action thereon.

When a battalion operates against battalion the colonel should prepare the problems and act as umpire. If he does not do this the practice should not be omitted, the majors concerned must get up their own although this is not so satisfactory.

The battalion commander or colonel should give a critique after each exercise, pointing out all errors of tactics and of exe-

cution. There should be much more of
tactical instruction and less of mechanical **Hints for**
training in battalion work than in the com- **battalion**
pany. **training**

Majors should not be limited to these drill periods to instruct their officers but be allowed to have tactical walks at other times. A major should have a good knowledge of tactics, be able to give clear and concise orders and enter into the spirit of his work. Four good companies, under a competent major learn with very little practice to work together as a team and become an efficient battalion.

THE REGIMENT

In the period alloted to the regiment the
solution of tactical problems and thereby **Regi-**
the gaining of experience in team work and **mental**
imparting tactical instruction to the officers **training**
are the ends sought. The same rules as to method of control, giving of orders and critique apply as in the case of the battalion.

The colonel is responsible for the training of his regiment. It is not trained until the three battalions, the band, machine gun platoon and mounted detachment are trained, each in its special work, and then the whole is practiced as a team.

The training of the twelve companies, as such and as battalions, has been discussed.

Band The band forms a large part numerically of the sanitary detachment of the regiment in battle. It must be trained and made efficient. This should be done by the officers of the Medical Corps serving with the regiment. There should be no perfunctory performance of this work; the colonel should see that it is thoroughly done.

Machine gun platoon The officer in command of the machine gun platoon must not only instruct his men in the care and working of the guns, but in the proper care of all his equipment, including the animals. The machine gun is an emergency weapon; the commander of the machine gun company must thoroughly understand the tactical use of this weapon and be able to act as circumstances demand even without instructions.

Mounted detachment The mounted detachment must be trained as scouts.

Objects sought in regimental training The principal objects sought in the regimental period are practice and experience by the colonel in handling his regiment as a whole, practice by the regiment in team work, and tactical instruction for all. A practical knowledge of tactics on the part of the colonel is essential if these exercises are to be correctly carried out and his critique of value. Overlooking tactical errors in these exercises does much harm, younger officers gain wrong ideas and it is hard to eradicate errors once firmly fixed in the mind.

Objects sought in regimental training

If the different units of the regiment are separately well trained it requires few exercises to make a team of them, good regimental work is largely a question of the tactical skill and ability of the colonel. If he is competent and the units are separately well trained the regiment is trained. Placing these well trained units in the hands of an incompetent regimental commander is but placing a fine and complicated machine in the hands of an unskilled operator; there is a fair chance that he will ruin the machine.

V

ARTILLERY FIRE

Object of study of artillery

EXCEPT in small engagements in detachment warfare the infantry will have the assistance of friendly artillery and will be opposed not only by infantry but by artillery fire. Some knowledge of artillery, its use, the effects it can produce and how best to utilize the aid afforded by our own and to meet the opposition of the enemy's, is therefore necessary for the infantry officer and also for the men in ranks. While familiarity with the artillery will be far from breeding contempt, it will enable the infantry to escape much unnecessary loss and, by correcting the false conception so many have of its power, it will improve the morale of our men.

This chapter is not intended to teach infantry officers what they should know about artillery and its use. It is offered merely as a suggestion as to what our men should be taught and how to train them to meet certain phases of this fire. The officer should know much more about the subject and must go to more extended works by more competent men for the instruction.

Artillery is effective against infantry both physically and morally. The moral effect is the greater, the less instructed and trained is the man. Most untrained men have very exaggerated ideas as to the effectiveness of artillery, they know nothing but guess much. It is the terror of the unknown.

There are two general classes of artillery that accompany an army: light and heavy. The light artillery may be rifles or light howitzers; the first have a flat trajectory, the others, of greater caliber, have the advantage of being able to use high angle fire. Mountain and horse artillery are merely subdivisions of the light artillery and, except that the mountain artillery is less effective at long ranges than the others, "all look alike" to the infantry advancing under their fire. **Classes of artillery**

The heavy field artillery in our service comprises 4.7" and 5" rifles and 6" and 7" howitzers. Their range is much greater than that of the pieces of the light field artillery. In a general way we may say that these heavy pieces will be used only against hostile batteries, earth works and material objects or against troops caught in some mass formation. They will generally not be used against an advancing skirmish line or troops in proper formation to meet light artillery fire. There is no training to be given infantry except discipline to hold them to their duty in an earth work under fire by heavy field artillery, hence in this chapter we may ignore it.

Light artillery   With light field artillery it is very different. The light field artillery is what concerns us most in our training. The extreme range for which these guns are sighted is 6500 yards, and at all ranges under 5000 yards they can produce serious losses on infantry exposed to their fire. They use two classes of projectiles, shell and shrapnel. The high explosive shell has a much smaller radius of action than the shrapnel, but is very effective within this area. It is generally used to batter material objects and with high angle fire to get at men in trenches or behind cover.

Shrapnel   The shrapnel of the 3" rifle contains 252 bullets and on burst these bullets are scattered over an area, roughly speaking, eliptical in form, 200 yards in depth by 25 yards in width. The flatter the trajectory, the deeper becomes the pattern made; the width practically does not vary. In other words the 252 bullets are scattered on burst over an area of 5000 square yards.

If these bullets were uniformly distributed there would be *one* for every 20 square yards or an area of 15 x 12 feet. They are, however, not evenly distributed, being thicker in a small area near the front end. This bullet will not penetrate the infantry soldier's pack at any range, so that when lying on the ground his pack affords complete protection to his spine and considerable protection to all vital parts except his head. The chance then of a man being wounded by a single shrapnel, even when inside the cone of dispersion, would only be about 1 in 80 if in the open and very much less with partial cover, as a trench, log, etc. The shrapnel bullet will not pass through one man and wound a second as will the infantry bullet. **Shrapne**

While artillery can fire very rapidly once the range data is accurately determined it requires considerable time to get into position and determine this data. Until then it is harmless. **Rate of fire**

An erratically shifting target is hard for artillery to keep on. The fuze must be so set that the burst is at the proper height and distance to the front of the target to be effective, both not easy especially in case of a moving target, and the more erratic the move- **Moving target** ment the harder is the task of the artilleryman.

On the defensive

On the defense the man's protection is much better for he will generally have cover of some kind, but he has also a serious disadvantage, the line remains fixed, the hostile artillery soon locates it, gets its exact range and can place its own fire where it will do the most good. This is a decided offset to the defenders' diminished vulnerability. The use of high explosive shells by their moral as well as physical effect weakens any advantage the defense might have as concerns artillery fire.

Artillery targets

To determine the relative vulnerability of different infantry formations let us apply to them the target made by a bursting shrapnel. A line of skirmishers at the normal interval extending across this beaten zone would have 19 or 20 men inside its extreme limits; if in squad columns there would be 2 squads at least and generally 3 squads or 24 men and the target, being much deeper, would give the artillery a better chance as it is easier to get direction correctly than the point of burst.

In platoon columns there can be but one platoon in the same burst if fire comes from the front, and platoons are 4 squads strong, but the whole platoon may be within it. If, however, the direction of the artillery fire be very oblique, and the platoons are on a line, more than one platoon may be caught by a single burst but not all of any one column.

Artillery targets

In successive thin lines, if the advance be made by one man from a squad, and the fuze and direction be just right, there may be 2 men in the cone of dispersion, which is to say that, in that formation, the artillery has about one chance in forty of wounding a man. If the advance be by one man from each platoon the artillery's chance, provided range and fuze are correct, is one in two that one man will be within the cone of dispersion of a given shrapnel and, if in there, there is one chance in 80 of his being hit; in other words, the artillery has one chance in 160 of getting one man and no possibility of getting two. Such a target will hardly draw artillery fire.

An infantry battalion in column of squads well closed up can nearly all be covered by the burst of a shrapnel. Such a target would likely draw many shots as would a company in this formation.

We can only win in the attack if our infantry can advance to the hostile position.

The advance under artillery fire

We must get there, and as soon as practicable and with the least loss of life. We can not afford to lose too many in the advance or we shall be too weak at the end to drive the enemy from his position.

The infantry can not open fire until within rifle range of the enemy and should try to get much closer before doing so. In open country, however, infantry may be subjected to artillery fire while crossing the ground from 5000 yards to, say 1200 yards from the hostile position, with no chance to reply. The problem to be solved by the infantry commander is how to cross this zone without losing too many men and too much time.

In skirmish line

In skirmish line. The long advance in this formation is tedious work, and the target offered is sufficiently vulnerable to draw artillery fire. If no cover is afforded in the terrain the line is apt to suffer heavy loss and become more or less disorganized before reaching the point where it will take up the fire fight. Where the line of advance is crossed by ridges, sunken roads and other features of that kind affording cover, where the line can rest and to a certain extent reform, this formation can be used to advantage, especially if the terrain permits us to approach under cover from artillery fire to within two or three thousand yards. If this formation be used in a force of some size, as a war strength battalion or more, the platoons should not keep on a line but in an irregular echelon formation.

In skirmis line

This makes a much more difficult target for the artillery. The distance from front to rear between any two adjoining platoons should not be less than 150 yards. The advance in skirmish line has the advantage of being in the formation that it will be necessary to have when you open fire and no changes are necessary and, if the enemy is enountered much sooner than expected, you are prepared.

The squad column. This formation was devised by our soldiers at maneuvers at Sparta and in California, where the ground in part was covered with thick brush. It was found an excellent formation to take when the skirmish line encountered these patches of

The squad column

The squad column

thick brush. Since it was placed in the I. D. R. it has been understood by some as a good formation for advancing in the *open* against artillery fire. This is a mistake. It should never be so used. In this formation there will always be two squads, and generally three, in the burst of a single shrapnel, exposing more men to danger than if they were in skirmish line.

Marching in column of files is not as easy as in line on open ground. Remember good artillery is pretty accurate in getting direction. Most shots will be at the head of a column and if at the head of one, another on each side is included in the burst. Direction is much easier to get in artillery fire than exact fuze setting in the case of a moving target; this is another reason against the squad column, the target is deeper and thus slightly improves the chances of the artillery. This formation not only has no advantage on open ground, in an advance under artillery fire, but does have disadvantages.

Platoon columns

Platoon columns. In average terrain this formation will be more used than any other. The distance between these columns is great enough so that a shrapnel bursting between two may entirely miss both; it also permits a more or less erratic or zig zag course to be followed. Each column is lead presumably by a more intelligent and better instructed man than in the case of the squad.

Platoon columns

These columns should never be on the same line but echeloned as explained for the skirmish line.

In most terrains there are little hills, clumps of trees, buildings and other cover of the same general kind. Platoon leaders must while keeping generally within their own zones of advance, rush from one cover to another where it is offered and, where cover is wanting, vary the pace and avoid advancing in a straight line.

Properly done this formation is one of the best. No time is lost, the columns are far enough apart to allow of advantage being taken of all the cover afforded, and the target is not, on average terrain, too vulnerable. It is not so good on flat open plains and it should not be used on such ground if the artillery fire is very oblique to the line of advance.

This form of advance requires that platoon leaders understand the theory and also requires much practice on different sites to give platoon commanders facility in leading

Platoon columns
and skill in taking advantage of the cover offered. This is one of the things in which captains should give instruction during the indoor season with the aid of the sand table. In addition outdoor practice is most necessary. When this formation is adopted platoon commanders should know, if possible, before starting where line of skirmishers is to be formed.

Successive thin lines
Successive thin lines. This is by all means the safest formation on open ground in plain view of the hostile artillery observing station. The successive lines must be so far apart that no one shrapnel can reach two; this distance depends on the range but may be taken as 200 yards. With one man from each squad there will be two in the cone of a single shrapnel that bursts right; if the enemy is so situated that he can afford to fire at such a target and you do not want to pay the cost for such an advance, then send one man from each platoon in each line. Hostile artillery cannot afford to fire at such a target and if it does it will use up ammunition that will be much needed later and get small results for the expenditure.

The chief objection to this formation is the time it takes. In advancing in skirmish line or in platoon columns your firing line is established as soon as you get your first line up, while, with successive lines formed from squads, it takes the longer time required for a line to advance 1400 yards, and if formed from platoons it takes the time required for a line to advance 6200 yards.

<small>Successive thin lines</small>

This formation is also safe against oblique fire.

The training of the men for it is simple. Before the line starts the point where it is to be rebuilt must be carefully designated. That the line may be rebuilt without confusion or mixing, each man must be taught to keep his eyes on the next preceding man of his own squad or platoon to ensure his finding his right place in the new line.

After a few of the successive lines have reached the new position, they form a dense enough target to draw artillery fire. For this reason the position of the new line should be one affording cover from artillery fire if possible; if not, men must get cover by digging to protect at least their heads from shrapnel. Head cover and the pack will give them protection from being killed if not from being wounded.

If the advance in this manner must be for

three or four thousand yards and the enemy has advanced posts or is likely to make an infantry counter attack, the advance over this whole distance can not be made at once but must be made by steps, growing shorter as you approach the enemy's position.

Artillery sweeping fire   The artillery will often sweep with fire an area being crossed by infantry. This is done by increasing or decreasing the range after each shot until the entire area is beaten. If this process be repeated often enough the artillery will get anything within this area not under cover. But this does not change the average number of shrapnel required to get a man nor does it render advisable a great expenditure of ammunition for meager results.

Infantry encountering this kind of fire should, as it approaches, lie down and get what cover is available and, after the storm has passed, move on.

The artillery may determine the exact range to some zone which the advancing infantry has to cross and, as the infantry reaches it, open a heavy and accurate fire. The infantry must cross this zone in a formation which decreases its vulnerability as much as practicable, consistent with other conditions, such as the hostile infantry fire.

The enemy's guns can get you if they expend enough ammunition at the task; but can they afford the ammunition? Your own artillery may interfere with such an expenditure even if the enemy were willing to make it.

Artillery sweeping fire

A division deployed with 2500 men on the firing line, crossing correctly in thin lines a fire-swept zone from 4000 to 1200 yards, might lose 10% of this number from artillery fire and not have its advance even checked. With this open formation the loss is so small that the moral effect of it will be negligible with trained men. But a loss of 250 men at an expenditure of 160 shrapnel for each means 40,000 shrapnel. Even half that much would be more than could generally be afforded.

After the skirmish line is formed at the position for opening the infantry attack, the further advance from there is conducted as already explained. In skirmish line the hostile infantry is now by far your most dangerous foe, but the artillery will still be punishing you: your line must advance under both fires.

Forming skirmish line

Artillery fire will seldom be uniformly distributed along the entire skirmish line or continuous in its action. There will be blasts of intense fire, then a lull. The troops must

Forming skirmish line

be trained to take advantage of these lulls to advance and to lie quiet during the periods of hottest fire. Of course, if for any cause the artillery fire is not very effective, the advance continues as against the infantry.

Our infantry must be taught to keep their fire superiority over the hostile infantry and to this object to devote all their skill and energy, but to avoid unnecessary heavy loss from artillery whenever possible. The hostile infantry is their real opponent, their real danger. As the opposing lines get close the losses from artillery fire become relatively slight, compared with the losses from infantry fire.

How to practice advance under artillery fire

How are we to get this training in most of our posts where there is no artillery to afford us the practice?

A man with a red flag indicates the position of a hostile battery, or, if the battery is concealed, a position that can be seen and is in the general direction of the battery. When the flag is waved rapidly it indicates a rafale or violent burst of fire; waved very slowly, it indicates slow fire by battery. In most exercises no flag is necessary; the instructor can give verbally the direction from which the artillery fire is coming in stating the problem; but in practicing the attack formation, under combined artillery and infantry fire, the flags should be used to practice platoon leaders in the rushes under such conditions.

Infantry is sometimes detailed to support batteries that are somewhat separated from the rest of the troops and liable to attack by a rush of infantry or cavalry. Officers on this duty must thoroughly understand their mission. They must protect the artillery. Artillery can generally take ample care of itself if the attack comes directly from the front. The infantry commander must never mask the fire of the guns. Where he will place his men and what his general dispositions will be is a problem in tactics and the solution will vary with each case. These general propositions may be stated: his position must be such that from it he can effectively meet the attack; it should not be where he will get too much of the fire directed on the batteries; the command must be well in hand and the reconnaissance and observation groups so employed that he will have timely warning of the hostile approach and be prepared to meet it. His position will generally be to a flank and probably somewhat to the rear, never in front of the guns.

Infantry as an artillery support

Infantry as an artillery support

An occasional exercise in this work should be carried out as a maneuver. Something should be placed to represent the guns and a battalion or company assigned as their protection while another force is given the mission to capture them. This exercise should always be carefully umpired to see that the guns get credit for what they could do if fire is not masked. A problem of this kind is a small part of the work of infantry in war and when it comes it is a tactical problem like any other attack or defense. The reason for recommending it is that it affords excellent practice in security and information service and in combat when one position must be avoided. Combat exercises should be as varied as possible, here is another variety.

Fire superiority

The importance of fire superiority has already been dwelt upon as well as how much the effectiveness of hostile fire falls off as the effectiveness of our own increases. Infantry alone does not gain this fire superiority but it gains it by the help of our powerful ally and sister arm, the artillery.

Artillery fire over infantry

Battle fronts are too short for the artillery to occupy space in the line, even if this were a good place for it which it is not; it must fire over the infantry. All our men must be made to understand the effect of this artillery fire on the effectiveness of the hostile infantry, how much more effective this latter would be without the fire of our artillery, and the importance of having this artillery fire kept up to the last possible moment. Prove to them how much less we shall lose by an occasional premature burst than we should lose by the increased effectiveness of the hostile infantry if our artillery ceased to fire. The men must be taught that it it is the infantry that does most of the killing and that, especially at the very short ranges, we want all the help we can get to keep down this killing by the enemy's infantry. *Artillery fire over infantry*

It has already been shown why the attacker's artillery has an advantage—the target is fixed. If the men are properly taught this there will be no trouble in getting them to want the artillery to fire over their heads as long as possible.

The connection that must be kept between the infantry commander and the commander of the batteries told off to his support is of the greatest importance, but that will be the function of a higher ranking man than this book is written for. *Tactical connection*

How part of this instruction is to be given

has already been told. It is believed that the best way to give the theoretical part is in small doses between exercises in the field—the little talks referred to before. Care must be taken not to give too much at once and to continue explaining until the men really grasp it. The theory should go along with the practical work; some of it can be best given in the non-commissioned officers' school and, as before stated, on the sand table.

How to instruct

How and when you do it is of less importance than *that* you do it.

VI

PATROLS, ADVANCE AND REAR GUARDS, OUTPOSTS

PATROLLING. The great importance of this work calls for the most careful instruction being given our men in this duty. It is not easy to teach, there is so little of it that can be done by thumb rule except in the simpler forms as visiting patrols. The first requisite is that the instructor know the subject thoroughly. As this work is in no sense a treatise on tactics that phase of the question will not be entered into here.

In teaching this subject in the company the following course has been found to give good results. In the winter's school thoroughly instruct all the non-commissioned officers and selected privates in the fundamental principles; for example, the various formations, the necessity of the leader's determining his mission and knowing how to interpret what he sees, how to write a message, and how to decide many other questions. *Teaching patrolling*

With this oral instruction there should be work on the relief map or sand table. This latter is one of the most important aids in teaching this subject. The instructor with a *Sand table work*

Sand table work small group at the table gives a simple situation and then, turning to one of the men, gives him an order as patrol leader to make a certain patrol on the ground represented by the map. Allow a short time for the section to think it over then question the leader. First get his idea of his mission and plan of action, question the others as to what they think of it, then the instructor gives his idea or concurs in that already given by the men.

Next the leader should be required to tell what he would do up to the time of moving out, the inspection he would make, what men must have and what they must not have, all the instructions and information he would give his patrol. The other members are called on in turn to point out any errors or omissions, then this part is discussed. The leader then points out his general route and gives the formation of his patrol along this route under the supposition that no enemy is encountered. The others are questioned as to their ideas of the correctness of the leader's decision.

The instructor should then take up the march in detail, something as follows: When you reached this point what would you do? How would you get from here to there?

When you reached the bottom of this little hill what did you do? And so on, bringing out carefully and thoroughly how woods, bridges, defiles and villages are traversed, etc. *Sand table work*

At the conclusion the instructor should go back to the start and at various points along the route have them see various hostile patrols and bodies of troops, bring out what should be done in each new situation, what messages sent, whether by one man or more, whether written or verbal, requiring in every case the reasons. The problem should be worked out once on the assumption that the patrol is in hostile territory and once as in friendly territory, the instructor bringing out clearly the difference in conduct. The mission should then be changed, as for instance from a patrol seeking information change the problem, on the same ground so as to give it a mission of screening.

The various phases of patrolling, in friendly and hostile territory, with a mission to gain information and then to prevent the enemy's gaining it should be worked out carefully on the same ground with only the necessary changes in the problem to bring out the differences in their conduct. It seems to impress these differences on the men the

Sand table work

more lastingly, the more closely the problems resemble each other in other respects and when they are on the same ground.

After this series is once worked through with the men, other problems on different ground are taken. It takes considerable work of this kind to make the men proficient in the principles of patrolling. As soon as they are deemed proficient they should be taken out for tactical walks in patrol problems on the ground and there given problems to solve, the instructor acting as umpire. This is all work that can be done in most posts in the winter season by taking advantage of the most favorable weather for the outdoor part.

The instruction in the principles of patrol leading can be given to better advantage on the relief map or sand table than on the ground but the latter training can not be dispensed with, some of it must be given. Later on there should be much opportunity for further practice in the course of the combat exercises.

Other kinds of patrolling

The work of the expeditionary patrol should be taught in the same manner. The work of the visiting and connecting patrols can be taught during the exercises in advance guard and outposts. They require very little effort. The company as a whole should be frequently exercised as a strong patrol. There is one form of patrol, often very strong, that is of great importance and yet its proper training is frequently neglected—the combat patrol. These patrols are always thrown out when a command deploys for action and upon their proper conduct much depends. Their mission is always to prevent the firing line from being unexpectedly fired into from the flank and they fulfill this mission according to the situation, either by securing the flank by themselves holding off the enemy, or by observing and giving timely warning so that the support or reserves can be disposed to meet the enemy and thus ward off the attack. *Other kinds of patrollin*

It must be thoroughly impressed on all what the mission of the combat patrol leader really means and that any position or formation of such a patrol, that allows the firing line to be so attacked is all wrong.

The following must be thoroughly taught:

1. That when the patrol is so situated that it can see no more than the men on that flank of the firing line it is serving no valuable purpose. *The combat patrol*

2. That in practically all cases where it

The combat patrol

is not in advance of the firing line it will not gain the necesary information in time to be of any value.

3. That the enemy must not get within effective rifle range of the flank of the line.

The strength of the combat patrol must depend on whether it is merely to observe or to offer real resistance and its conduct must be governed accordingly.

It is believed that the principles governing this work can be best taught, after a talk in the school, by a form of tactical walk, where the instructor can devote himself to the handling of this patrol; later on it is, of course, practiced in all battle exercises.

Combat patrol tactical walk

In the conduct of such walks the instructor takes his class out as such patrol and states his problem, the firing line being represented by a few men or even entirely imaginary, its progress being announced from time to time. The instructor then acts as leader, explains what is to be done and, assuming he has a platoon, takes his first position. He conceals his platoon and has observers out covering him and so placed that any enemy approaching will be seen in time, and that he will be in the best position to meet him. The number of sentinels out and their distance from the main body of the platoon depend on the terrain. He then carefully points out his dispositions to the class and explains why made and assuming in turn that the enemy is approaching from each of the likely directions, how his dispositions enable him to meet fully the case. The necessity for signal communication with the commander is explained and how he has provided for it.

<small>Combat patrol tactical walk</small>

He then discusses the terrain with reference to the next advance. As the firing line advances where he should next go, and how get there. A small patrol advances to the next position selected, finds it unoccupied and so signals back. The platoon then moves there and sentinels are sent out as before and possibly small reconnoitering patrols. The same discussion as before. Also from time to time hostile patrols are assumed to be seen and what should be done explained; when fire would be opened on the main hostile line, if at all. In fact the whole conduct of this patrol until the conclusion of the fight should be discussed, showing how it jumps from place to place, always covered by sentinels or small patrols, and how the firing line is always protected by it from surprise. He should point out how, in most cases, a mere marching along

Combat patrol tactical walk
in a straight line would utterly fail, and impress upon the men the fact that the leader must use his head all the time.

Having gone through such an exercies once or more, the instructor solving the problem himself, he should then prepare the problem and, having stated it, call on the class to solve it step by step in the same manner. In all cases of errors in disposition the instructor assumes an enemy from a certain direction and has the class realize the error by their inability to meet the situation. The importance of keeping as many of the patrol as practicable well in hand must be emphasized.

Any combat patrol that is to offer resistance, from a squad to a company, is handled in the same way. The work of the smaller combat patrols whose duty is only to observe are likewise taught in the same way. The terrain and conditions bringing about their use instead of the larger ones make the problem easier.

The officers of the battalion should be taken on such walks by the major or some other officer. The company commander should conduct them for his lieutenants and non-commissioned officers.

The men should also be practiced in the same way, as the combat patrol or covering detachment of a defensive line. This work is simpler, the patrol generally does not move from position to position. Its mission is the same as in the attack and even more important. In the defense very much depends on the selecting of the best position for this patrol and the correct dispositions being taken.

Combat patrol tactical walk

The case must be also considered of a patrol sent out by the defense for reconnaissance or screening which in case of attack becomes the combat patrol.

In a battle line with intervals, as in the case of the enveloping attack, connecting files must be used. Their object is to keep the commanders of the subdivision informed as to how the other is progressing. This can generally be done by forming points in the line joining the two inner flanks. In some cases this will not serve. Rules for this can not be given.

Advance Guard. In most commands too much of our limited field training period is devoted to work of advance and rear guards. It is important and must be taught, but if the other work which is the real foundation for

Advance guard training

Advance guard training

this is properly done but little more time is required outside of the maneuver exercises for training the enlisted men. Patrolling and combat form most of the work in these exercises so far as the men are concerned.

There are many tactical problems that come to the officers in this class of work and they must know how to solve them. This is the work of the school for officers and should be effectively done.

Advance guard rencontre

The point is but a patrol with a special mission. The flanking groups are reconnoitering and scouting patrols but they involve some new features. When a recontre engagement occurs on the march one of the first things the commander wants to know is the strength of the enemy and his location; if deployed, where is his line? Where its flank? If not deployed, what is he doing? As the advance party deploys and pushes on, these flanking groups have the best opportunity to observe and by reconnaissance to gain valuable information. They also become, temporarily at least, combat patrols to the firing line. The men must be taught to carry out this mission without further orders and to do it correctly. In case small detachments attempt to delay our march, these patrols by flanking them can greatly hurry their retreat and prevent the delay of our column.

The general principle of advance and rear guards should be taught the company. This work can de done in part at the relief map and sand table, but the company should be exercised on the ground as the advance guard of a battalion and as the advance party of a larger advance guard, the other troops being imaginary. Afterwards two companies should work against each other, one as rear party of a rear guard, the other as advance party of an advance guard; also each as advance party in a rencontre.

Maneuver work

If the foundation has been properly laid there is no difficulty in teaching the application of these principles to covering detachments. If it has not been so laid and the men do not thoroughly understand patrolling in its different forms, it will be hard to teach it in these exercises.

In maneuver exercises problems involving rencontre engagements and engagements involving a marching column encountering an enemy in position should be had to train the officers in tactics and to give the men practice in combat exercises and in the patrolling necessary.

Outpost training	Outposts. The general principles of outpost duty, the duties of sentinels, the general formation of an outpost line with its subdivisions must be taught the men indoors. The officers have much to learn in school or from books on this subject. With proper preparation by all the work outside is simple.

There are a few things that need special mention:

In the instruction work have a definite situation. If the company is to be exercised as a support take an outpost order giving the situation and general location of the supports. If any detachment, including the company, is to march beyond assumed existing covering detachments, see that it is properly covered by an advance guard. Judgment must be used in this, the smaller the detachment the weaker relatively the cover. Bear in mind where the other detachments are marching and the amount of cover they afford to yours.

When starting out instruct the advance where you are going, then have it go far enough in advance of that to cover you while you are making your dispositions after you have reached your destination.

From the company down make the distribution of troops and assignment of tasks in an orderly manner, much as the guard is divided up for the post guard; do this while the detachment is still formed. **Outpost training**

Full information of the situation should be given the men; the proper performance of their duty is impossible otherwise. Each subdivision commander must attend to this. The captain should give as much of the necessary information as practicable to the whole company, this saves time for the picket commanders and will probably result in the situation being better understood.

Where the outpost line should be located and how it should be disposed varies with many conditions. It is a tactical problem that the officers must be able to solve and must learn elsewhere than on the ground in the few hours devoted to this work in troop training. **Outpost practice on the ground**

A little practice should be held by the regiment as a whole in forming outpost; one with the regiment as the outpost and one with the regiment as the whole command, one battalion forming the advance guard on the march. In the latter, a halt order should be issued and outpost formed from the advance guard battalion; when completed a march order should be issued by which the new advance guard passes through the outpost line. The outpost should then be assembled and take its place in column.

We do this very easily in map problems; try it on the ground, especially in rather close country.

Mounted scouts
The mounted scouts. While the mounted scouts have been taken from the infantry regiment there is still with each regiment a mounted detachment of orderlies. A few mounted scouts well trained are invaluable to an infantry regiment when operating alone. The commander of an infantry regiment, if wise, will see that these orderlies are trained as scouts and then when necessary he can so use them. Their most important and frequent use will be as the mounted point and flank patrols for an advance or rear guard and for patrolling to the front of an outpost line.

To be of any value they must be well instructed in these duties as described under advance guard. Being mounted they are much more valuable than a dismounted patrol for gaining information from the flanks and getting it back to the commander in time to be of some use. These orderlies can be trained in this work without interfering materially with their instruction in the care of horses and equipment and it can be given along with instruction in horsemanship.

VII

MARCHING

ABILITY to march under war conditions is of primary importance in the training of infantry. There is much more marching than fighting in war and, no matter how well a man may be trained otherwise, if he is unable to reach the field of battle he is of no value as a fighting man.

Requisites for marching

That the infantry soldier may be able to meet the requirements in this respect he must possess the necessary health and strength he must be properly shod, know how to care for himself on the march, especially how to take care of his feet, and his muscles must be properly developed. It is also necessary that the responsible officers know how to conduct the march and to care for the men.

That the man has been allowed to enlist presumes the possession of the necessary health and strength and gives us a man who can be trained to meet all necessary requirements except when temporarily sick or disabled.

The soldier's shoes must be of proper

construction, well fitted to the man and the leather kept soft and pliable. The shoe now issued to our army is good and with proper care in fitting leaves little to be desired. The fitting of the shoes is an important duty of the company commander and should never be slighted. The rules prescribed for this should be carefully followed. Every captain of infantry should have and carefully study the little book "The Soldier's Foot," by Lieut. Colonel Munson, Medical Corps. *Shoes for marching*

No matter how well a shoe may be fitted if it becomes soaked with water and dries, without proper care, it will become hard and stiff and sore feet are apt to result. The men's shoes in campaign should be kept oiled. Neatsfoot oil should always be carried in every company's baggage and officers should see that it is used as needed. There should also be a supply of talcum or foot powder.

The socks are of nearly as much importance as the shoes. They, too, must fit. If too large they wrinkle, if too small they are apt to bend and injure the toes; in both cases the result is sore feet. Woolen socks are much better for hard marching than cotton, they keep the feet dryer and afford more of a cushion and consequently better *Socks for marching* protection from injury. If the man finds that wool next his skin produces too great irritation he should wear woolen socks over a pair of cotton or lisle thread.

Care of abrasions

After a day's march the feet should be washed and any blisters and abrasions should receive proper attention. Adhesive plaster should be applied to all such, even to spots that are sore and the skin not yet broken; properly applied it is a great protection.

Rather than have the men treat their own feet it is much better that, after the day's march and camp has been made, a reasonable time be given the men to wash their feet and prepare for inspection. Captains should then carefully inspect the feet of all their men and send every man with the slightest injury to the regimental infirmary at once and have the injuries properly treated.

Men should be taught to do this for themselves but as it can be so much more surely and better done as above described the men should be permitted to do it themselves only in emergencies where sanitary troops are not available.

Protection of head and neck

In marching in very hot weather the men must be instructed in the importance of protecting the back of the neck from the direct rays of the sun. It would be well if our men were issued a small piece of cloth of suitable color with some means of readily attaching it to the hat to afford this protection. The Japanese soldiers used such an attachment in Manchuria with good results. *Protection of head and neck*

There must be an air space between the top of the hat and the man's head. The hat must be ventilated and in very hot weather a wet sponge or cloth or green leaves should be carried in the hat. The shirt collar, if not very loose, should be unbottoned.

Besides bathing the feet the men should bathe their whole bodies frequently. Anyone familiar with our "regulars" on the march and who has seen them break for the water to bathe as soon as possible after a day's march knows that it requires no order to get this done. But sometimes we must camp where there is no water available for bathing. Men should at least wash the crotch with a wet towel, especially if there is a tendency to chafe. Talcum powder should be used in such cases. *Bathing*

Men should be carefully taught the disabling effects of alcohol if drunk the night before or during a hard march, especially if the march be made in hot weather. The men must also be instructed to care wisely for their diet and to avoid the excessive drinking *Drinking*

Drinking
of water on the march. Too little water is as bad.

Personal hygiene
All this instruction should be carefully given the men by their company officers under the general supervision of the regimental surgeon. The surgeon, with the approval of the colonel, should prepare an outlined scheme for instruction in first aid and in personal hygiene, having special reference to the soldier's care of himself in the field. The surgeon should then instruct such company officers as have need of the instruction; the company officers then instruct the men. A part of the examination of the company at the end of its indoor period should be on these subjects.

Muscle development
The muscles must be *properly* developed. It is not the strongest man who can best stand the march; it does not require great physical strength. The man's muscles must be flexible, he must be trained to use them and be able to use them without causing physical pain.

Marching as fully equipped infantry in the ranks is a very different proposition from walking along the road independently, and for the private in ranks with his load it is different from what it is for the officer with his.

Many men of great strength are often what is called "muscle bound." Others have certain muscles overdeveloped others underdeveloped. When muscles usually unused are brought into play, or when a man is forced into a constrained position, if it be kept up continuously for some time, serious pain and discomfort results and often ends in a physical break down. **Muscle development**

A good course in callisthenics or in gymnasium training is the best thing for the new man. It loosens him up, brings into play the different muscles, renders them flexible and gives the man control of himself. Then practice in marching, carrying his equipment, strengthens the necessary muscles and accustoms the man to the necessary constraint.

The training of the company for marching consists, then, in getting the men's muscles in proper condition by physical drill, in theoretical instruction as outlined above, and actual practice. Most of the actual practice is and should be gained at the regular daily drills and exercises. In these, if they are properly conducted, the man gets enough preparation. **March training**

Devoting one day each week to a practice march is believed a mistake. In many of our posts a command going out on the roads can **Practice marches**

Practice marches

not leave them, there is no chance for instruction except very imperfect instruction in advance and rear guard work and practice in marching.

The physical part, the mere practice in marching can be just as well gained in the regular exercises, and to devote one-fifth of our field training period to the other instruction is excessive. It prevents some of the other necessary training being given and it ignores relative values.

What are wanted are men physically fit. Four to six hours a day of correct and rational training will make them as much fit without this weekly practice march as with it and give more time, all of which is needed, for necessary work.

Yearly march

There should, however, be one march every year of from 200 to 300 miles. This is necessary for instruction in camp expedients, to train the men to care for themselves on long marches and to give them experience in field service.

It would be better could it be held late in the season. The command should march to come point where they could have maneuver work and training in the larger units and on the ground more unfamiliar than their home reservation. But the march should be held, if it be only out and back.

Even with the men well prepared much of the success of the march depends on the officers. They must understand how to conduct a march and care for their men and conscientiously perform their duty. They must try to get the man's point of view, think of the man's comfort and health. *The officers*

Every officer who may be responsible for the uniformity and rate of march should carefully train himself to take a suitable gait and strictly maintain it. No one thing is more trying than an unsteady pace and many good officers are unable properly to lead a column on on the march for this reason. The halts must be regulated to suit conditions. In very hot weather or when climbing steep hills they must be more frequent than once an hour. *Marching gait* *Halts*

Discipline must be strict, no straggling allowed. Running to catch up, "backing and filling" is productive of a big sick report.

Whenever conditions permit the intervals between units should be increased, especially when the weather is hot and roads dusty. It renders a steady, uniform pace easier to maintain, and thus tires the men less.

The other rules for marches given in our

service regulations should be carefully observed.

The first few days Much of the success of a long march depends on the first two or three days, until the men get into the swing. Where practicable the first day's march should be a little less than average, the second a short one, after that our trained regulars can keep up the average march six days a week. On starting out it is the second day's march that is the most trying to the men. This should be borne in mind and all practicable allowances made.

An excessively long march should never be made just for practice. It does not fit the man for another but the reverse.

VIII

THE NATIONAL GUARD

IN training the infantry of the national guard we have a very different problem from that of the regular regiments.

In these regiments the same proportional attention should be given to those things that should be habits as in training the regulars and the necessity for varied instruction in order to keep the interest of the men is even greater.

My observation leads me to believe that the greatest weakness of many of our national guard captains lies in the narrow scope of the instruction given and in its monotony. There is a lack of variety at each meeting. The men lose interest. *Scope of the instruction*

When the recruit first joins the guard he generally does it for the best of reasons and is interested in the work. But after going to the armory for a few times and drilling in a few movements over and over again he loses interest, then he cuts drill and possibly ends by trying to get discharged.

There are many things that should be taught, and you can only hope for success by varying the work and holding the interest of your men. Do not put more time than necessary on non-essentials.

The recruit
Of course the recruit must first be taught the school of the soldier and he must have the necessary instruction in close order drill. But even early in his course there is a chance for variety; early in the game give him a rifle for part of the time and as soon as he has had a little drill in the manual of arms teach him sighting and then pointing and aiming drill. As soon as he is far enough along let him fire a score at gallery practice each drill. At first devote the most time to drill without arms but increase the time with arms until all the drills are with arms and you get him in the company for close order drill.

The following should be taught as carefully as practicable:

Essentials for the guard
1. Target practice on the range. If the gallery practice and pointing and aiming drill recommended below be well done, comparatively little of this will answer. But it cannot be omitted, every man should have some practice. Where possible some of this practice should be in "field firing." In many

cases there is a tendency to give known distance firing an exaggerated value to the neglect of other training.

Essentials for the guard

2. The mechanism of the deployments, the advance by rushes even after the line is mixed, control of fire, and all these directed by signals only; verbal commands should not be used.

3. Estimating distance must be taught.

4. Pointing and aiming drill and gallery practice, so that the man will always bring his piece up properly, look through the sights and pull the trigger only after careful aim, must be practiced until the necessary habit is formed.

5. There must be frequent close order drill. Knowledge of this is necessary for the orderly movement of troops and it is our greatest aid to discipline. But to be an aid to discipline it must be exact, otherwise it has a reverse effect. It is just as easy to do it correctly as to do it approximately if you only teach it so at the beginning and then give the subject attention ever afterward and do not allow the drill to become sloppy.

6. The use of the bayonet must be taught and practiced.

7. The men must be taught simple in-

trenching and the various uses of sand bags.

Essentials for the guard

8. First aid and personal hygiene.

9. Patrolling; especially the combat patrols and those with advance and rear guards and outposts. As many as possible should know how to read a map.

10. The company musicians and two or three privates should know the flag signalling.

But the captain may say: all these are practicable with the regulars who have all the time needed and daylight in which to work and ground to work on; but how are we to do these in an armory at night?

Required equipment

Every armory should have a place fixed for gallery practice if it is only a backing for the target against the wall in one of the corners. And no company should be without a sand table; a relief map is also very desirable.

With this equipment let us see what we can do.

The ordinary drills of course are on the armory floor.

Estimating distances

The principles of estimating distance should be taught the company and the men urged to practice it for themselves. Groups are formed and go anywhere it is convenient for this purpose. Occasionally, if found practicable, the company goes out. Officers and non-commissioned officers in this same way should learn to use the range finder.

Patrolling can be well taught on the sand table or relief map. Pile up your sand, forming any desired terrain; with yellow strings mark the roads and with blue ones the streams, little bridges, etc., can be made with a jackknife, houses represented by blocks, forests with little pieces of evergreen—you have your outdoors. **Patrolling**

A scale must be provided and one end of the table marked as north.

The instructor takes a squad to the table and starts out, for instance, by stating: "Smith, your regiment has reached this point (just off the table) moving north in hostile territory. The colonel sends for you and gives you this order—'Corporal, I have heard rumors that there is a force of the enemy in that village northeast of here. I want to know whether that is true. Take your squad and move along in the general direction of this main road, find out and report. The regiment will remain here for several hours. Be back here by 3 P. M., it is now 10 o'clock.'" The instructor tells Smith to do just as if he were on the ground. Smith inspects his

Patrolling squad, gives his instructions to his men and then proceeds. He can tell the instructor his formation, and what he does from time to time, or each of the men, provided with a match and a scale, may be required to move his own match. There are many ways of doing it. The instructor must give information of the enemy, either orally or at certain points place lead soldiers or something to represent the enemy.

The thing aimed at is to find out how Smith and the other men would act under various conditions, point out their errors and show them how to correct these, and give the reasons. An infinite number of such problems can be devised.

This sand table is especially good for teaching the work of a combat patrol. Form your field of battle and along one flank have a varied terrain with houses, clumps of trees, little hills, etc. The instructor moves a light rod along to represent the firing line and the patrol leader solves his problem. Whenever any error is made the movement stops until the mistake is pointed out and explained.

Security In the same way are treated advance and rear guards of the strength of a company and a company as advance or rear party. Outposts are established, the sentinels being represented, and routes of the patrols selected.

Entrenching can be taught by constructing trenches to scale on the sand table terrain. I have seen elaborate field works with bomb proofs constructed in this way by the men of one company, but this is not recommended for any but the officers; it is better to limit this work to the simpler trenches. With a round piece of stove wood for a log and with a good jack knife, or better a hatchet, you can make your loop holes for the head log. With a lot of small Bull Durham tobacco sacks, filled with sand, you have your sand bags, the varied uses of which should be taught. **En-trenchin**

The officers should have a war game map for their patrol problems and for war games.

Bayonet fencing should be practiced if you have the necessary equipment. If not, and a place is available for it, suspend by a rope something to represent a man, a sack full of straw will do, so that it can be made to swing through a small angle back and forth and to right and left. Let the men practice the thrusts, lunges, cuts, etc., against this, another man giving the dummy a motion. This should come after training in the bayonet exercise. **Bayonet fencing**

I would propose a system something like the following for your company drills:

Recruits by themselves until they can be put in the company; their work has already been discussed.

Essentials at every drill

After the company is formed give 15 or 20 minutes of snappy, precise close order drill then a little manual of arms. Then have the company deploy, two or three times at least, from different formations. Then go through an attack formation the best you can, all the company in the line, no support, an advance of 40 yards being represented by one of five, etc. Then try it holding out a support and putting it in so as to mix squads and advance as before. Remember, no verbal commands, all this to be done by signals.

Have little posters on one wall of your armory at the proper height; have a few minutes pointing and aiming drill, impressing on the men the importance of always taking careful aim.

Group work

Then divide your company into small groups. One group at the sand table, one receiving first aid instruction, another bayonet work, another gallery practice, etc. The group at the sand table may be larger than the others and may stay there for the rest of the evening, the others should change every 15 or 20 minutes. The sand table group should change each drill and once during the night if practicable, that is, if there is time for one group to finish its problem and give another a chance that same evening, it should be done. Nearly all the company should fire a score at the gallery every night.

<small>Group work</small>

If there are a few men in the company who are poor at the manual of arms they can be put in one group and be given one of their turns in drill in the manual.

One group may have to be taught how to make the pack. Instruction in guard duty may be necessary for another. Verbal instruction can be given in several subjects with great advantage where a good instructor is available; in that case all except the group at the sand table can be assembled.

The whole course cannot be covered at one drill. The captain should so arrange his groups that all in turn get instruction in the whole course, that all get a variety each night, that where men have a special deficiency it receives attention, that the first part, the essentials for the whole company, be never slighted, and that as many as practicable of the company get gallery practice at every drill—one score will answer fully.

Group work

Owing to the time it takes to complete a problem or task on the sand table, often but one group can use it in an evening. The size of the group working should not, however, be increased. Only small parties can be advantageously instructed. For this reason the sand table must be worked to the limit and because of this and the number of things to be taught on it and because some officers are not very expert in forming suitable terrain on the sand table, it is an advantage to have the relief map also. The latter can then be used for patrolling and work of covering detachments and the sand table for the field engineering.

Brush work

At most stations small twigs can be collected and used to make hurdle revetments, fascines and gabions for use on the sand table. They can be constructed to the reduced scale and this brush work learned nearly as well as outside with normally sized faggots.

Have the officer or non-commissioned officer best qualified give the instruction in each class. The instructor has much to do with success; some are specially good at one thing but poor at another.

With such a course of instruction well given throughout the year and with a week or ten days of good camp work annually, and suitable school work for the officers, there is no reason why the national guard should not possess the efficiency required of it to be a valuable military asset.

Sufficient of the callisthenic or setting up exercises for the proper development of the soldier should be shown the recruit and the latter told of the advantages of practicing them for a few minutes every morning or evening, or both. Tell him what it will do for his health and appearance and urge him to get busy. There is no use drilling these exercises in the armory. A few minutes once a week or less often will do no good and wastes drill time of which the guard has none to spare. *No callisthenic drill*

The detailed sergeants should help in all drill work but especially should be valuable in teaching camp expedients, care of equipment, etc.

I believe that in nearly every state the officers pursue a theoretical course each winter and generally there is a non-commissioned officers' school as well. In the latter school there should be thoroughly taught, giving importance and precedence in the order stated: *Use of schools for N. C. O.*

Infantry Drill Regulations,
Manual of Guard Duty,

Small Arms Firing Regulations, and parts of Field Engineering.

<small>Use of schools for N. C. O.</small>

Parts of the Field Service Regulations should be read carefully in connection with the study of the same subject in Infantry Drill Regulations. If more time is available map reading should be taught, and, if time remains, then applied minor tactics on the map. Attempt no more than you can *thoroughly* do in the time available and make the course progressive.

<small>Schools for officers</small>

The school for officers should first cover thoroughly the above course but take more of Field Service Regulations and include the Manual of Courts Martial. Map reading should be thoroughly learned by all and the remaining time put on tactics. Beginning with minor tactics study some good problems with their solutions, then solve others to be criticised by some competent person. I have found it satisfactory to use problems in this way in connection with the drill regulations. Study a subject, for example an advance guard, then read a few tactical problems on the same subject, then try solving one, and so on.

As you progress use larger and larger forces. But do not attempt the brigade until you can handle the regiment correctly. Do not cover too much ground in one season and acquire only confusion. Each term get something positively fixed in your mind so that you can use it; there will be more winters.

Schools for officers

Much attention should be given to acquiring facility in giving correct verbal orders.

Studying tactical problems correctly solved and solving others for yourself is the best way to learn tactics after you know the principles laid down in your manuals. Beware of "normal form" solutions, they are misleading and apt to be wrong. Apply general principles with common sense. Advantage should be taken of the officers detailed as inspector-instructors to plan and conduct this work as well as to help in the instruction of the men. Only those thoroughly competent for this instruction work should ever be detailed with the national guard.

There should be a camp of instruction each year. If properly conducted this is very valuable.

Nearly all national guard infantry needs training for individual men and officers and work in the company, battalion and regiment. When formed in divisions or larger

Camps of instruction

Camps of instruction
forces for maneuver campaigns the men in ranks and junior officers get but little instruction. Except a little camp experience, it is chiefly walking, the object of which they know nothing, and most of the officers are not yet ready for this class of work. It is a camp of instruction, not a campaign, they need. They must apply on the ground what they have learned in the armory.

I believe the best results can be obtained from camps of not more than three regiments The special needs of each regiment should be considered in forming the program. The work should be planned so as to give instruction to each in the most important things in which it is deficient. Special consideration should be given to what can not be learned in the armory and must be done out of doors.

Most of the program should be made up of practical drills and exercises in which all get instruction from private to colonel, and where their interest can be held and the best instruction given. Small maneuvers of company, battalion and regiment are what are needed.

Tactical walks for officers and non-commissioned officers are an excellent means of instruction—these supplement the other exercises.

The big maneuvers are very largely for general officers and very little for regimental officers. We need the foundation before we build the superstructure.

Camps of instruction

As much ground should be covered during the camp as is consistent with efficient instruction. No attempt should be made to cover the whole art of war in a week as it only results in confusion of ideas and gives little or no benefit.

If the law would permit a few national guardsmen to serve for short periods in the regular army it would help greatly towards uniformity of training and improve the non-commissioned personnel of the guard. These men should be allowed to so serve for three months during the company's field training period or for one month during the indoor season; not more than five should be assigned to any one company. They should receive the regular's pay and rations and, if joining for the three months period, one complete service uniform; the one-month men should bring their uniforms with them.

Service with regular companies

This privilege should be granted only to men who have still one year more to serve in their enlistment in the guard and who are recommended by their captains. They

Service with regular companies

should be excused from post guard and all fatigue duty and in place of that receive additional instruction work each day. In order to obtain the most benefit, these men should be attached to those companies whose training is the best; in an indifferently trained company they would get some benefit but it would be little in comparison with what they would receive in the other class.

This recommendation is made from having recently seen the results of having a few men of the national guard join an excellent regular company for a short period. These men came without pay and themselves paid their board while with the company.

There would probably be no large number who would so serve, but there are some and we are in no condition in this country to overlook even small helps that will contribute towards fitting us for war.

Value in war

Owing to the small peace strength of most of these regiments and the large number of recruits they must take in on the outbreak of war, their value will depend on the time they will require to be fit for the field at war strength. They have the organization in working shape. Their officers will, in the majority of regiments, be men who have had considerable training. If they will follow a logical and systematic course of training in peace, the officers will be familiar with it and will be experienced instructors, and all their old men will have the instruction to a certain degree so that they can help drag up the recruits. All this will help to shorten the time required to fit them for the field and every day thus cut off adds greatly to their value.

Value in war

Without such training their value is small, for no regiment should be accepted except at war strength and a national guard regiment so filled up, without experienced instructors who know the course, will take nearly as long to become efficient as would a new regiment.

IX

INSPECTIONS

MUCH can be done to improve the training of our infantry by the inspections. Most officers greatly dislike to have an adverse report made by an inspector on their commands. Fear of such a report sometimes works to the detriment of sound training and sometimes to its improvement.

Influence of inspections

A captain once asked why he put so much time on exercises of obviously little consequence and so little time on others more important, replied: "Blank will inspect this year. He always pays great attention to such and such an exercise and never examines the company in the others. I want a clean record on this inspection."

We have all been influenced as was this captain. Even if we do not care personally, loyalty to our colonel or to the post commander leads us to consider what the inspector will require.

The author has no intention of criticizing adversely the Inspector General's Department; its inspections have steadily improved in recent years and become more rational and consequently more beneficial. His aim is rather to point out the place of the inspections in the year's training and to suggest how, in connection with the methods of training proposed, they may be made both searching and helpful toward real proficiency.

Influence of inspections

In the annual inspection it is evident that in the time available the inspector cannot examine an organization in everything it should know; he must choose certain things and judge from those of the training of the company or regiment.

The annual inspection

In making this choice the relative importance of the subjects must be kept in mind. Of course every company must be tried out in the combat exercises and in all the things that should be made fixed habits. It is of equal importance that no stress be laid on non-essentials. For the rest, he should select certain important things which every company should know and inspect it thoroughly as to its proficiency in those, examining the various companies at a post in different subjects so that a captain would feel that anything in the whole course might fall to his lot from properly making the pack to establishing an outpost at night.

The annual inspection

The inspector should make free use of the war game map, tactical walks and every other recognized means of instruction to find out how well the officers and men of the regiment are instructed and what class of work each organization is doing.

In order to be fair to the organizations inspected the annual inspection should be made late in the season. It should never be made before the officers have had a fair show to instruct their commands.

Company examination

The above inspection by an officer of the Inspector General's Department should not, however, be the only one. At the close of each period of training there should be an examination of the organizations on the work they are supposed to have done. The last of March or first of April the field officers of the regiment, as a board, should examine the companies on the results of their winter's work; a similar examination should be made

Battalion examination

at the close of the period of company field training. When the battalions have finished their period of field training the colonel and lieutenant colonel should form the board to examine them. If the brigade commander be thoroughly posted on all matters pertaining to infantry training his presence at the examinations and careful supervision of the work cannot fail to be very beneficial. His supervision should not, however, lead to restriction of the proper latitude which should be allowed subordinates; his mission should be to see that the instruction given is correct and that the whole course has been satisfactorily covered.

The same general principles apply to the inspection of national guard organizations. If anything is found wrong with them the inspector should not keep silent at the time and content himself with rendering later an adverse written report; he should tell the officer being inspected what is wrong and take pains to show him how to correct the error. A helping hand, offered in the right spirit, will always be appreciated.

<small>National guard inspection</small>

X

TRAINING A NEW REGIMENT

Need for quick training IN this country we are liable to have the necessity forced upon us of turning out troops in the shortest possible time. We shall have to use troops not fully trained; we shall have to employ them as soon as they can be used at all. Of course this system will be frightfully costly in blood and money. In war imperfectly trained troops must pay with their lives for all mistakes. The better trained they are, the fewer mistakes, the more skill they possess the more cheaply can any desired result be obtained.

It is the duty of all officers who may be charged with the responsibility of preparing this mass of untrained men for war service to give the subject careful thought, to study the question carefully and to be prepared on short notice to take charge of such work and produce the best results possible in the shortest time.

Success in this hurried training can only be secured if the man in charge thoroughly appreciates his task and follows out a well prepared and systematic course.

There are three phases of the problem: Our regular regiments must be raised from a strength of about 65 men per company to nearly 150. The national guard regiments, less well prepared, will have, as a rule, to stand a still greater increase of new men, and there will be hundreds of entirely new regiments to be raised.

In outlining or suggesting a possible course to be pursued in such cases let us take the new regiment. The regiment must first be enlisted, organized and equipped. This first step will not be considered further than to say that in its organization it is absolutely necessary that its commander be an active, competent officer, one who can train it and prepare it for its work. In no other way can the regiment be prepared to do anything within a reasonable time.

The commander

To appoint an incompetent commander to such a regiment would cost many lives, would be a crime closely resembling murder in the second degree.

An effort should be made in every new regiment to have a reasonable number of subordinates competent to act as instructors.

General Principles Training

Under modern conditions there is a minimum amount of training that is absolutely necessary before an organization can be put in the field. The number of men lost to an organization from disease depends on how well the men are trained in caring for themselves and how well the officers do their part.

Time is the all important element; we must have these organizations in such shape that they can be used as quickly as possible and be as nearly good as possible. Of course they will constantly improve in the field and become excellent, but they will have to be used before that state is reached. The occasion for organizing such regiments will only arise in case of great national danger, when the utmost can be demanded of all. Hours of work should then be all that can be profitably employed. Most of the recruits will be men accustomed to at least eight hours work a day.

All that has been said previously as to variety in the work, keeping up the men's interest, explaining and giving the reasons for things done, applies even more to a new volunteer regiment than to our regular companies. Essentials only must be taught at first, bearing in mind that discipline is most essential and the use that can be made of close order drill in obtaining it. Those things that should be a habit must be drilled carefully and frequently. Other essentials may be hurried through for the first time, to give the men the best general idea possible in the shortest time, and then repeated and perfected as time and opportunity offer.

<small>General principle of training</small>

As a rule our men will be intelligent and quick to learn. Every little taught them, if they have understood the reason for it, will help them to do what is required even if their instruction is not complete. With such volunteers much instruction should be given not as a drill but as a sort of lecture or talk. The average American works better when he knows the why and the wherefore. Remember how different are his new life and surroundings from what he is accustomed to and how very little the average American knows of an army and how much of that little is not so.

In submitting a proposed schedule of training it is fully appreciated that conditions will vary greatly and any schedule must be suited to conditions as they exist; it is doubtful if the one here proposed would ever exactly fit. It is only offered as a possible help.

It is assumed that the colonel is thoroughly competent and that there are several men in the command with some military training, such as ex-regulars and national guardsmen and those who have had training in a college battalion. This latter assumption is a safe one in this country.

Company cooks

It is very probable that every company will have a cook that enlisted as such and knows something of the art. But handling the ration and army cooking have features that are different from what he is used to unless he has been trained in the army. The company kitchen must be correctly run or training will be difficult. Discontent and a big sick report are fatal to success.

The first thing, then, is to instruct the cooks and mess sergeants. Some one must be found competent to do this and he must look after the kitchens, correct mistakes and give instruction until they are all running properly. The new captains must learn how to look after this work properly if they do not already know. If the colonel can find nobody else to do it he must do it himself. It must be done. It is a very important part of the foundation upon which success must be built.

The necessary records and papers should be properly kept and made, both at regimental headquarters and in the orderly room. This is important but not so much so as the kitchens. The mistakes in paper work only cause annoyance and confusion off the battlefield and possibly will lose somebody some money; but the other causes loss of life and prevents efficiency. This work should be properly taught. Some competent non-commissioned officers or officer should be given the task of instructing the clerks and first sergeants. It is not difficult, at least the essential parts, and it should be promptly attended to upon organization but so as in no way to interfere with training. An ex-regular sergeant major, first sergeant or clerk would be very valuable here. So far as possible such a man should be made adjutant of every new regiment of volunteers. His value as an instructor in many things would be great and he would save the colonel much trouble and annoyance.

Paper work

From the first day of training the band should be turned over to the surgeons for thorough instruction as auxiliary sanitary troops. At least two hours a day should be devoted to this work until they become

Band

proficient, after which, an hour or two a week, to keep them so.

Band The band must also receive the necessary drill so that it can be maneuvered as such. Callisthenic drill, practice in marching, care of themselves in the field, individual cooking, and tent pitching must be taught. Three hours daily should be devoted to this instruction until satisfactory results are obtained, after which only occasional drills are necessary. This may interfere somewhat with their music, but that can wait.

Surgeon The regimental surgeon must also carefully train his detachment. His officers must not only be doctors but medical officers; his men must be trained for field service as well as for hospital attendants.

Machine gun company The training of the machine gun company and mounted detachment must begin from the start and follow generally the lines proposed below for the companies. More attention must be paid to their tactical instruction than even to that of company commanders. They must know their function **Mounted detachment** and how to do their part. The instruction of these men as to field service, care of themselves, callisthenics, cooking, etc., must be the same as in the company. They must be taught how to care for the animals and in the case of orderlies how to ride and to scout.

The company musicians will receive the following instruction with their companies: callisthenics, first aid and personal hygiene, individual cooking, tent pitching and rifle firing. They make all practice marches with their companies. They will be grouped by battalion and given at least one hour a day of instruction in signalling, and the musicians of the regiment assembled under the drum major for instruction in the necessary marching and maneuvering and practice with their instruments. They should work about the same number of hours per day as the other men. {Musicians}

Those armed with a revolver must be instructed in its mechanism and care, and firing practice frequently held.

In the proposed schedule given below for the companies an effort is made to provide for the necessary muscular development referred to before. The amount of this drill is not as great as desirable but as the men progress bayonet exercise and pointing and aiming drill answer fairly well to supplement this work. Some will object to any callisthenic drill, under the assumed conditions, {Callisthenic drill} as a waste of time. They are wrong—it will save time in the end, keep down the sick report and give better results.

<small>Instructors and drill masters</small>

The colonel should carefully inventory his command for instructors and drill masters. In the early stages when divided into small groups many are required; fortunately but little military training is necessary for this preliminary work.

Owing to shortage of good drill masters groups for this preliminary work will have to be larger than is customary in peace time in the regular service, not less than eight men to a group from the start, and these should be combined into groups of two squads each then into platoons, as soon as their work permits. The best instructors should be kept as drill masters after each consolidation.

For the callisthenic drills from the very start the men can be combined into large groups and instructors found who are already competent to drill their squads in the school of the soldier. The other squad commanders who are imperfectly prepared must be assembled at this time for drill and instruction under the best officers and non-commissioned officers in the regiment. They will be carefully taught the next movements to be given to the men and how to teach them to their squads.

As these squad leaders are selected as far as possible from those having had some military training and the others from the brightest and most intelligent men, it is believed possible for them to keep ahead of their squads. It becomes easier as the groups grow larger and fewer instructors are required.

Instructors and drill masters

The drill will be given to the officers who do not know it. The officers being formed into a squad by themselves.

All trained officers must be on the drill ground during all these drills by squad, supervise the work, correct mistakes and help out the poorer instructors. The other officers not acting as instructors should be required to attend about half to learn from seeing it done, the other half of this time they should be required to be drilled themselves and to study the drill regulations. There should be no hesitation in having lieutenants drill squads during this period provided they are better at it than some of the enlisted men and are not needed to supervise the work of several squads.

There should be an officers' school every evening except Saturdays and Sundays.

Officers' school

This should be conducted by the colonel himself. The first subject taken up being the drill regulations. Lessons should be short as well as the sessions of the class and the work thoroughly done. The student officer must learn the text and the instructor fully explain it where necessary. Much explanation will be required in Part II.

The class must keep well ahead of the outdoor work.

Besides the Infantry Drill Regulations, in this school must be taught early in the course, parts of the Guard Manual and Small Arms Firing Manual. The essential parts of the Field Engineering will be taught, and, those not proficient therein, how to read military maps. Lastly take up the Manual of Courts Martial.

The more important parts of Army Regulations should be included in the above course. Better results will be obtained if the lesson each day includes two or three selected paragraphs from this book than by taking it up as a whole and by itself. In its use this is largely a book of reference. In this proposed way the officers become familiar with it and how to use it and the relatively few paragraphs they must positively know are learned.

If, beside the colonel, the regiment has three or more thoroughly competent officers, the colonel will not require the others to attend officers' school but will order schools for non-commissioned officers with these others as instructors. The classes should not be larger than one composed of all the non-commissioned officers of a battalion and, if instructors are available, those of only two or three companies should form a class. *N.C.O. schools*

The work of this class will be largely confined to Infantry Drill Regulations. First the drill then combat and covering detachments must be fully explained and the principles of patrolling taught. If time is available these schools will also take up other subjects taught in our regular indoor course. Care must be taken not to give the men more in one lesson than they can learn.

If there be one, and less than three, competent instructors for these non-commissioned officers, a class will be formed in each battalion and only two sessions held weekly for each, the instructor taking them in turn. Lessons in this case may be longer but the work cannot be so well done.

If there be no one available except the colonel, each captain will be required to have

N.C.O. schools a school in his company at the most convenient hour and try to transmit to the men what he has learned in the officers' school.

The following instruction should be given by demonstration or by talks given to the men assembled and sitting.

Talks and demonstrations Part of it will be given by battalion, part by company, 2 and 4 should be given by squad or platoon, the leaders having first been instructed. In the schedule this instruction is designated by the word "verbal". Its value will depend on the instructor.

List of subjects for instruction by talks and demonstrations:

1. General duties of a soldier. His relation to his officers. System of discipline. Military courtesy. Customs of service as they relate to him. An outline of organization. Encourage the class to ask questions on the subject in hand and kindred subjects and then answer them.

2. The rifle, its mechanism and care and how to clean it.

3. Care of the other equipment, especially that of leather.

4. How to make the pack and adjust it.

5. Duties of a sentinel on the interior guard. Sentinels' orders.

6. The most essential parts of the course in personal hygiene and first aid.

Talks and demonstrations

7. Importance and necessity of fire control and distribution.

8. Instruction as to artillery with a view to diminish unreasonable fear of its fire.

9. Principles of patrolling.

10. Objects of advance and rear guards and outposts.

11. Duties of a sentinel on outpost and conduct of visiting patrols.

12. If time is available give more instruction under 6.

Most of this is only preliminary to explanations and instruction the men will get in their drills. It is a start, and at the beginning of his training will help to arouse interest and gives some variety at the time when, in the regular drills, but little variety is possible and the drills are least interesting. A good instructor will make this pay.

It is assumed in this schedule that the season is between May and October. Work beginning on a Monday.

Reveille at 6 A. M. Breakfast immediately after. Necessary police between that and 7 A. M. No drill Saturday afternoon except one hour for instructors; none on Sunday.

PROPOSED SCHEDULE
1st, 2d and 3d Days.

A. M.

1st week
6–30	to 7–45	Drill for instructors and officers only.
7	to 7–30	Callisthenics.
8	to 8–45	School of the soldier without arms.
9	to 9–45	Same.
10	to 10–30	Callisthenics.
10	to 10–45	Drill for officers and instructors.
11	to 11–45	Verbal.

P. M.
1	to 1–45	School of the soldier without arms.
2	to 2–45	Same.
3	to 3–45	Same.
4	to 4–30	Callisthenics.
4	to 5–00	Drill for officers and instructors.
7		School to last from $\frac{1}{2}$ to $\frac{3}{4}$ of an hour at first, later the time to be extended.

4th and 5th Days and Morning of the 6th
Day. **1st week**

The same as above except that the drill from 9 to 9–45 A. M. and 2 to 2–45 P. M. will be in the manual of arms.

Some camp guards will probably be necessary. This should be done by platoon and this time on guard used to the utmost to teach this duty.

2d Week.—During this week drills will be in the school of the soldier without and with **2d week** arms, the proportion with arms steadily increasing.

Commencing Thursday one-half hour each half-day will be pointing and aiming drill.

    A. M.
6–30 to 7–45 Drill for officers and instructors.
7–00 to 7–30 Callisthenics.
8–00 to 9–15 Drill—school of the soldier.
9–30 to 10–15 Verbal.
10–30 to 11–45 Drill.

    P. M.
1–00 to 2–00 Drill for officers and instructors.
1–30 to 2–00 Callisthenics.
2–15 to 3–45 Drill.
4–00 to 4–30 Callisthenics.

4-00 to 5-00 Drill for officers and instructors.
7-00 School.

3d week.—Squads combined in pairs. Drill will be with arms. Part of each drill will be pointing and aiming drill and extended order, close order work being continued. Beginning Thursday an aggregate of half an hour daily will be given to bayonet exercise. The drill must be varied, change made every 15 or 20 minutes.

A. M.
7-00 to 7-30 Callisthenics.
6-30 to 7-45 Drill for officers.
8-00 to 10-45 Drill.
11-00 to 11-45 Verbal.

P. M.
1-00 to 3-45 Drill.
4-00 to 5-00 Monday and Wednesday—estimating distance.
Tuesday and Thursday—intrenching, using the small tools.
Friday — Instruction in guard duty by company.
7-00 School.

4th Week.—Squads are combined into full platoons. Five or six men are selected from

each company to form the signal detachment
of the company. These men are required to 4th week
do at least one hour's work a day at this from
now on until thoroughly proficient, and excused from a corresponding amount of other
work, preferably police and close order in the
afternoon.

A. M. 7 to 11 DRILL	Each drill to be divided approximately as to time as follows: 30 minutes pointing and aiming drill. 20 minutes bayonet exercise. 1 hour close order drill. Remainder of time extended order drill.
11 to 12	All non-commissioned officers have gallery practice and instruction in use of range finder.
P. M. 1 to 4 DRILL	The best officers of the company for the work take one-half the non-commissioned officers of the company for work in patrolling. The two sections alternate as to days. Remainder of company will be divided into groups. All must have gallery practice at least 5 shots per man

P. M.
1 to 4
DRILL

daily. Only one group at target at a time. Each group to have estimating distance twice during week. Each group to have individual cooking twice.

Each group to have one hour's instruction during week in first aid and care of feet on a march.

All to be taught to form for and pitch shelter tent camp.

If the necessary masks and plastrons are available practice in bayonet fencing at least three times during week for each group. If no fencing rifles are available, poles the length of the rifle and bayonet, with a good pad fastened on the end, answer the purpose. If masks are not available bayonet exercise and close order drill will fill up the rest of the time.

In arranging this work the best man for it should be put in charge of each class of work.

4 to —

Company formed with full kit, except rations and ammunition, and marched first day about twenty minutes, lengthening the time each day by 10 minutes.

7 P. M.   School.

5th Week.

A. M.

7 to 11   Drill same as last week.
11 to 12 Same as last week.
          Gallery practice same as last week.
          Patrolling same as last week.
          First aid, same as last week.
          Estimating distance, once during week.
          Bayonet fencing or exercise for at least one hour during the week.

P. M.

1 to 4   Each platoon to be posted as a picket of an imaginary outpost line and men instructed twice during week.
          Each squad as above once as a sentry squad.
          A wall prepared and men given instruction in scaling it.
          Any time left over to be used as thought best.
4 to 5   March with pack as before, giving instruction in advance and rear guard.
7   School.

6th Week — Company.

6th week
Company

A. M.
7 to 11
DRILL
One hour close order, remainder extended order drill. Much practice in attack as explained in Chapter IV.

11 to 12 Same as last week.

P. M.
1 to 4
Gallery practice as last week, except on Friday.
Friday whole company as support of an outpost, sentinels and patrols carefully instructed.
Each non-commissioned officer, twice during week, to conduct a patrol, instructing privates.
Bayonet fencing and wall scaling as last week.
Estimating distance as last week. Remainder of time teaching men brush work, hurdle revetment, fascines, etc.

4 to 5 Same as last week.

7 School.

Saturday, formal inspection by company.

7th Week — The Company.

7th week
Company

A. M.
7 to 11
DRILL
As last week except that time given to close order may be reduced to 15 minutes daily.

7 to 11 DRILL	At least two days must be given to maneuver of company against company.	7th week company

All the men must fire 20 shots during the week at gallery practice at such times as found practicable without interfering with the prescribed program.

P. M.
1 to 5   Monday. Outpost, company as a support.

Friday. Practice march with instruction in patrolling, advance and rear guard, and attack and defense, either one company to work against another or enemy to be outlined.

Estimating distance drill while out. Men must not march more than 10 miles nor less than 6. Packs will be carried.

Tuesday, Wednesday and Thursday.

1 to 3–30 Patrolling at least once during week by each non-commissioned officer as leader.

Remainder of time to brush work, filling and piling sand bags, making loopholes and intrenching.

P. M.   Drill in dark as training for night
9 to 10   work.

School as last week.

Saturday, formal inspection by company.

8th Week — Battalion.

A. M.   Drill by Battalion. Not more
7 to 11   than one hour of this time per day should be devoted to close order. Gallery practice, same as last week.

P. M.   Tuesday and Thursday.
1 to 5   March and instruction by battalion similar to that by company last week. Distance marched about 10 miles.

Monday.

1 to 5   Tent pitching and making camp, including the large tents.

Wednesday and Friday.

1 to 3–30   Field engineering.

Work same as last week.

9 to 10   Night drill.

6   Monday, Wednesday, Friday, battalion dress parade. Each battalion once during week. School as usual.

Saturday morning, battalion review and inspection.

9th Week. Target practice on the range with ball cartridges.

9th week target practice

If the pits are not large enough so that each company can have three targets, only part of the companies should go at a time so as to give that number of targets. It should be completed by end of 9th week and may have had to come earlier for some companies.

If the range is right at the instruction camp it would be much better to have the companies shoot only a couple of hours a day beginning with 7th week and reduce the other instruction by that much, but so that at the end of the 9th week the work accomplished is the same.

10th Week.

A. M.

7 to 11   Battalion drill all but 15 minutes daily, extended order work. Battalion against battalion at least twice.

10th week

P. M.
1 to 5   Monday, battalion outpost instruction.
Wednesday, march by battalion with packs. Instruction as before.

Tuesday and Thursday from 1 to 5 and Friday from 1 to 3 instruction by company. Gallery practice, pointing and aiming and estimating distance, each once. Bayonet work for one hour. Wall scaling once. Two patrol problems for each non-commissioned officer. Balance of time field engineering work as before.

Friday 9 to 10 P. M. Night drill by battalion.

Battalions in turn have battalion dress parade on Monday, Tuesday and Thursday.

Saturday morning battalion review and inspection.

School, 7 P. M.

11th Week.

Regimental work. Colonel uses it to best advantage.

One afternoon practice march. Regimental dress parade 4 evenings. School, 7 P. M. as before.

Saturday, regimental review and inspection.

12th Week.

A seven days' practice march under war conditions with as much instruction as possible in field service, care of men, especially the feet, and of course in loading wagons, making and breaking camp.

12th week practice march

Marches, especially the first two or three, must not be long.

13th Week.

Work each forenoon from 7 to 11-30 in what, by careful observation, the colonel finds is most needed.

13th week

No work in the afternoon except as follows:

Each man to have gallery practice once, ten shots. Each man to estimate distance once. Companies to have bayonet work for at least two half-hour periods each week and pointing and aiming drill once for some length of time.

Dress parade by regiment three times during week.

Regimental review and inspection Saturday.

School as usual.

Results of training

This regiment can be used at the end of this three months. It will not be completely nor even well trained but it is believed to be the best that can be done in that time.

Can we have even this much time without great sacrifice and loss? It is very doubtful, and yet it is not believed practicable to use volunteers with less training except in fortifications.

The work has been very strenuous for all; the weaklings will have been eliminated. Any one fit for a soldier in war could have stood the strain, and the others had better be eliminated before taking the field.

If at the end of our 13th week we find we have more time, the work for the week following should be reduced to three hours per day and the schools, after that we may resume the long days of work.

XI

RECRUITING

THE method of recruiting has a decided influence on effective training. It is much harder to train a company whose recruits dribble in a few at a time than one, all of whose recruits for the year come in at once.

The best results can be obtained if these recruits can all be had in the fall. As stated before, the course of instruction should run from November 1st to October 31st. In the indoor season all that part of the instruction course that can be given, should be. It should be preparatory to the outdoor work. The foundation of sound training should be laid during this season; the recruit can then be given his elementary instruction and be ready to begin the outdoor work with the company. The outdoor season is none too long in which to go through properly the whole course of work that should be taught outside. *When recruits should join*

If recruits are received late in the spring or summer they are not prepared to do the work with the company, they get only part of it and that in a way that does not give good results. It is like trying to teach Algebra first, then Arithmetic. Another drawback to this method is that it results in the captain's not having all his company for this outdoor work. Our present peace strength is so low that correct training in parts is difficult and when much below this the training is very imperfect.

<small>When recruits should join</small>

Most, if not all, good captains very much prefer to have their recruits directly on enlistment to having them go to a depot for several weeks. The training they receive in these depots, in value, is out of all proportion to the time spent. In their companies, from the very start, while learning the recruit drill they are learning much else of value. The recruit is better off and more contented. In his company there is a personal feeling for him and interest in him not found at the depot.

<small>Recruit depots</small>

The instruction and ways of doing things first learned are those of his company, not always the case at the depot. The few movements taught at the recruit depots must be taught exactly right if precise close order drill is to be had, it is harder to change a recruit's ways of doing anything than to teach him the right way from the start. It has been suggested that if the depots are kept up, all drill thereat except callisthenics be prohibited. *Recruit depots*

Recruits dribbling in, waste effort. It is as much bother to a company to train and get one recruit into the company as a squad of eight. The large number of men held at these recruit depots would give a very desirable increase in strength to our companies if we could have them. The vaccinations that are attended to at the depots could just as well be done at the posts.

The following is offered as a plan of recruiting that it is believed, would improve that branch of the service and greatly improve the training of our infantry: *Plan of recruitin*

All recruiting stations and recruit depots in time of peace to be abolished.

Each regiment in the U. S. to be assigned a permanent district within which its recruits are to be found. The regiment may never be stationed inside this district but its recruits are all to come from there.

Early in November of each year, each regimental commander to select a few recruiting parties composed of an officer and three or four men from his regiment to beat up this district for recruits. They should visit the small towns as well as have stations in the larger ones. Before enlistment the recruits to be physically examined by a doctor, either of the Medical Corps or one hired in the district.

These recruits are to be sent directly to their regiments in detachments as enlisted and their training commenced.

As there are many young men who will not enlist for service in the U. S., but do want to go on foreign service, each home regiment will, in addition to getting its own recruits, be given the task of getting a certain number for the Philippines, Hawaii and Panama, the number being allotted by the War Department. Men reënlisting should be sent, as far as practicable, to foreign service. These latter will be sent to designated posts and held long enough to be properly equipped, vaccinated, etc., and then be sent to their regiments.

Large cities like New York and Chicago should not be assigned to a single regiment but three or four regiments to have stations there and part of the outlying districts to be theirs to beat up.

These recruiting parties to remain out until they have completed their quotas then to return to their stations, but never later than February 1st.

This plan offers several advantages and some disadvantages, but is believed to be an improvement. *Advantages of plan*

Its advantages are:

All the recruits of the company come in at one season and that the best one.

They come directly to the company on enlistment.

Companies can be larger without increasing strength of army.

The officer enlisting them belongs to the regiment as does his recruiting party and will exercise more care to get only suitable men.

The recruiting will be more widely distributed and as the men go back to their homes knowledge of the service, and trained men in case of war, will be generally distributed.

Fewer men from the slums of the big cities and more from small towns and rural districts.

The men of a regiment coming from one locality, year after year, a friendly feeling for the regiment should be built up and future recruiting assisted and, in case of a great war, every section will have its nucleus of trained men.

Discipline will be improved and desertion

diminished. The men will realize that their comrades are from their home section and people at home will know of their misdeeds. Besides it is pleasanter for the men to serve with those they have known before.

Advantages of plan

It cannot be asserted without a trial that this method will be cheaper than the present one but the author believes it will be.

To send out these recruiting parties will be a considerable expense but to offset this there is the cost of the present recruiting stations for rent, the difference in the cost of commutation paid and actual cost at posts, the travelling expenses incurred sending recruits to depots, often in an opposite direction from that to their future posts, the costs of keeping up these depots, a large amount, the loss of the service of all the recruiting personnel for any other valuable purpose during the year as well as the cost for the time lost in training of all the recruits.

The recruiting parties sent out by the regiments are taken from trained men at the season when they can be best spared and probably they would be absent but for a relatively short time.

If this plan be adopted the method will work better each year. The men who have

RECRUITING

gone back, and even those in the ranks, can and will help in the recruiting, and as the number of these increase recruiting will be more easily and quickly done. Each village will know that the party will visit it at a certain season and many will be ready at once.

Advantages of plan

It will be more expensive the first year or two than afterwards. The saving on deserters should be large after the first two or three years.

There are two apparent objections. That there will be no large number of recruits in hand to be sent to particular regiments in an emergency. This is of small consequence. Where the regiment is wanted for a sudden emergency, the adding of a large number of raw recruits is of no immediate advantage.

Discussion of objections

Suspending recruiting February 1st may result at first in some regiments not being filled up but this is doubtful. Most of our original enlistments at present are made in winter, and this would be offset, if it does occur, by the other advantages enumerated.

Convenience of administration and keeping records should have no weight as against efficient training for action, the only reason for our army's existence.

Possible modification

If the infantry cannot have the above system the following modification would improve matters.

Each company to receive recruits but once during the year, each in its turn and regiments as nearly at one time as practicable. The recruits to be sent out within one week of their receipt at the depots except those for foreign service. If the peace strength of the companies be kept at 65, when the company is assigned recruits it should be filled to a strength of 80 it will then average about 65 for the year possibly a few more. It is not believed the total enlisted strength of the army would be increased at all. It would amount to having the men with companies instead of in recruit depots.

The above will enable the captains to do much better training and greater efficiency will result.

Of course those who receive their recruits in October or November would have a great advantage over the others but all could do better work.

Recruits enlisted in summer could be held much longer than others and then, about September 1st, sent to the regiments stationed in the tropics. It is more comfortable for the recruits if they can reach those stations in the fall and get their first hard drills and become acclimated while weather conditions are most favorable. This would give the regiments at home their recruits at a favorable season if not the best for all of them.

Either of the above changes can be made by a change in regulations and orders.

Need for a change of system

With our great population and military needs and very small army it is folly not to use what army we have so as to be as well prepared for war as conditions permit.

In the preceding chapter it has been shown how important it is that we have some trained men for every new regiment. We must have trained men to fill the regular army which must bear the brunt of the first attack.

The present law does not provide this. The enlistment law should be radically changed to get the best results for training, general efficiency and preparedness for war.

All men should enlist for 5 years. At the end of one year's honest and faithful service, except when serving beyond the limits of the U. S., the man should, on his application, be granted a furlough for the remaining four years; if war breaks out, or becomes so imminent as to call for mobilization,

Enlistment law

Enlistment law

these furloughs to cease and the men to rejoin. The men to have the privilege of remaining on in the service if they so desire and of taking their furloughs at the end of any completed year of service. Discharges not to be given the men until the end of their full five years. Hence these men can not reënlist in another organization while on furlough, and there can be no doubt of their status and liability for punishment as deserters if they fail to rejoin when called.

Men on furlough

For the present, men should not be *required* to take the furlough and reënlistment should not be prohibited, but remaining in service with the colors over two years in time of peace should not be encouraged; later, if found practicable to get sufficient recruits, reënlistment for all, except non-commissioned officers and certain mechanics who first enlist after that date, should be prohibited. Men who have enlisted with the understanding that they can remain in service until retired, provided they behave themselves properly and are physically fit, should be honestly treated; they have an implied contract at the least.

Time on furlough not to count for retirement or increase of pay, and men on such furlough not to be counted in strength of company.

Recruits on foreign service should have the privilege of the furlough only after two years service, and men with regiments in the U. S. who wish to remain in the service, after one year's service should be encouraged or required to transfer to foreign service for the next two years.

<small>Men on furlough</small>

Men whose service in their first year has not been satisfactory and who are not fairly trained should be required to serve two years before being granted a furlough. The law should also provide that men, whose conduct is found unsatisfactory by a board of officers and the finding is approved by the colonel, may be furloughed at any time after two years service whether the man desires it or not.

It is believed the plan would work if no pay were given men on furlough, but if each be paid ten dollars each six months on reporting his address by mail to the adjutant of the post it would help in finding him when wanted and might be an inducement to some to enlist.

An effort should be made to get young men as recruits. Boys of eighteen or over if physically strong should be encouraged to enlist.

Young men are easier to train and for a longer time afterwards are available for service.

Men on furlough

We need a reserve but no men should be enlisted directly for it. The reserve for the regular service should be our men on furlough. Men too long out of service and advanced in years are not what is needed for the regular service which must be ready at short notice to face serious war.

The reasons for the foregoing recommendations as they appear to the author are:

Reasons for enlistment plan

1. Five years is as long as the average man is willing to pledge his future for military service unless he means to make it a life occupation. The latter class is not the best for the government. Young men are the best for the ranks in time of war. Men who serve only long enough to be trained for the work are to be desired. It results in a much greater number of trained men being available in time of war and is much cheaper, for it reduces current pay and the retired list.

2. The great importance of having as many trained men as possible and having them dispersed through the country to help in the formation of the new regiments at the outbreak of war is apparent to any one who thinks on this subject.

3. If recruits be received during the winter months only, the organizations can follow a prescribed course of instruction and complete it annually. If recruits dribble in throughout the year a proper course of instruction cannot be satisfactorily given in that time.

Reasons for enlistment plan

4. At the outbreak of war, it is of vital importance that we have as strong a force as possible of men fully ready trained and equipped. The losses at first in this force will be heavy. If green recruits, enough to fill the regular organizations to war strength and to make good the early losses, be poured in on them they will cease to be trained organizations. A reserve is a necessity. This will provide it at small cost.

5. Many excellent and patriotic young men are willing to serve a short time in the army for the experience and training. Four years, however, is longer than they are willing to postpone settling down to their real life's work. These are the men it is most desirable to get into the army, not as professional soldiers, but as a trained reserve for war. For the first years they are a reserve for the regular companies, then they become available for officers or non-commisioned officers

174 TRAINING INFANTRY

Reasons for enlistment plan

of volunteers. This class of young men will enlist much more freely when they can do so and lose only one year from civil pursuits.

6. Enlisting men as young as they are physically fit interferes less with their civil careers, hence will get us more desirable recruits. The physical and mental discipline a boy thus gets will help him in his future work and the younger he gets it, so long as it does not interfere with his schooling, the more it will be worth to him. Taking the recruit young, the five years while his military service is with the regulars are the five best for that purpose. Later when older, more developed mentally and matured in judgment he is best in higher rank than private with the volunteers. If he enters at 18 he is available at 23 for the volunteers or national guard and has at least seven years left in which he can be considered at his best.

7. The provision for letting men out at the end of one year, provided their conduct has been good and they are fairly instructed, will be a great aid to discipline and a preventative of desertion. A good many young men enter the service thoughtlessly and find after a few weeks that the life is different from what they expected. They look ahead to over three

years more of it and the weak ones desert. They are not vicious nor criminal as a rule but this step injures them seriously; they become prisoners or fugitives, and either will decrease the man's moral stamina and self respect. This provision will greatly reduce this. The man will see that he has only to behave himself for the rest of the year to return to civil life with a clean record. The great expense resulting from desertion will be largely eliminated. The men will be more contented, they will feel they can leave in a short time if they wish, which will tend to decrease the desire to quit. This does not prevent those staying in the service who wish to do so. A few old soldiers are desirable. *Reasons for enlistment plan*

Less than one year's training is not sufficient in which to cover properly the course the infantry soldier should have. Two years is necessary to make a good job of it. But we need more men who can be used in war. With some thoroughly trained men in the ranks it is believed better to have 100 others of one year's training than fifty of two or more.

The national guard should have the same period of five years for enlistment with a provision for inactive service, except in war,

Enlistments for the national guard — after two years of service, unless the man has had service in some other organization, as a college battalion. Less than two years is not enough training to be of value where so little time per year is devoted to it.

While it has nothing to do with training, there is another provision that should be in the enlistment law; that is, that every man who enlists for five years, and is in service when war breaks out, shall be liable for service for at least one year thereafter no matter when his term expires. At the outbreak of a great war is no time to discharge trained men.

XII

IN CONCLUSION

TIME is wasted at most posts on some things that are of little value compared with the time spent on them. *Relative values*

"Butt's Manual" is fine callisthenic drill and at proper times should be practiced. It would be just as valuable and even more so if, instead of having the men learn to go through it all without command, an instructor gave the movements and the men executed them purely for physical drill. The cadence amounts to little, but executing them so as to exercise properly the desired muscles is important.

Many captains spend a great deal of time practicing this so that their companies can go through the whole series without command and to music. It is pretty, and for the chorus in a musical comedy act might be a success, but for soldiers it is a waste of valuable drill time that could and should be put to better use.

Our inspectors have had something to do with this, and county fairs and similar shows, more. The narrow scope of instruction followed in some companies, and the seeking for the easiest way to kill the drill hour by a few, has helped to give this its prominence in our training.

Target practice Our target practice is open to criticism in some respects. Its importance can not be overestimated and it must not be slighted, but rational methods should be followed. It is necessary to appreciate fully what is required and wanted.

The individual man must be a fairly good marksman for two reasons: so that he can place his shots in a designated locality, and to give him confidence in himself. The better the men can shoot, other things being equal, the more confidence they have in themselves and in each other. For practical results on the battlefield an expert rifleman is of little if any more value than a marksman. Good, fair shooting by every man in the company is what is desired.

On the battlefield much depends on the confirmed habit, this habit-forming can not be done on the target range, but throughout the year's work. Not to exceed two weeks a year should be allowed to any company for known distance practice on the range. If its work during the rest of the year has been properly done, this is sufficient. The rest of the time is needed for other work. But the time put on field firing, where done in the solution of correct tactical problems, cannot well be excessive. The more of this the better. *Target practice*

The law granting extra pay to expert shots, sharpshooters and marksmen is not believed good in its effect; it gives undue importance to range firing. An expert rifleman without other training and discipline is of but little value on the battlefield, while even a second class shot, well trained and disciplined, is infinitely his superior as a soldier. This law should be amended so as to divide the men into two classes: the best men in each company to be rated as 1st class. To be so rated the man must be thoroughly well trained in *all* his duties, of excellent character and 1st classman or better in target shooting. The extra pay for 1st classmen to be so alloted as to cost the government no more than is now paid for higher classifications. Men have drawn this extra pay for qualification as shots who were of but little account as soldiers. *Extra pay*

Rifle firing among young men in civil life

Rifle firing competitions

should be encouraged. It is a necessary *part* of a soldier's training and is that much accomplished toward making efficient soldiers of them if the occasion arises.

Our rifle competitions take too much time and are allowed to interfere too much with regular training. Officers should not be allowed to compete. Their work during this season is with their companies; they should be learning the duties of an officer not that of the private in the ranks. It is undoubted that a man can not make much of a success teaching what he does not know. The officer must know how to shoot well enough to be an instructor, he must know the theory and have the knack of instructing. He does not need to neglect his regular work for weeks at a time several summers to acquire this at competitions.

The best company instructor in rifle firing the author ever saw on a target range was a first sergeant who himself never made better than marksman. The company was very short on sharpshooters and experts but was still shorter on 3d class men. The poorest instructor he ever saw was an officer whose breast on state occasions was covered with big medals for shooting. He had to spare his own eyes so as to make phenomenal scores; the instruction of the new men in the company was of little importance compared with the former.

The proper garrisoning of the army, to avoid so much necessary labor and afford better opportunities for training, has been given great attention by the War Department. May it soon meet with success. But much can be done even under present conditions to help in this matter. This beautiful parking perfectly kept is pretty, but it takes ground needed for other purposes and requires an immense amount of "fatigue" labor. This labor could be reduced: the parks would not be so pretty but military efficiency would be greater. For which does the government spend its money? **Proper garrisoning**

Our companies should be increased in size to 100 men in peace, in war to 150. Our companies are now too small for good training; it requires too many new men to raise them to war strength, and the present strength is wasteful of money and effort. **Strength of the company**

With the companies at a fixed peace strength of 65 it means much of the time still less. There are not enough men to drill in the regular platoon formations. In our extended

Strength of the company order work the captain is reduced to the capacity of a platoon commander and platoon commanders are out of a job. These men do not get practice in the handling of their proper units and it can not fail to diminish their interest and enthusiasm and result in poorer work as well as in incomplete work.

In the case of war we shall need our regular organizations very promptly and as efficient as possible. At the same time these organizations are certain to lose many officers taken for other duties. The addition of much more than one man to each two then in ranks, even if they have been previously trained, is a serious blow to efficiency. The new men must either be untrained or men from a reserve. If from a reserve they are rusty on many points and are apt to be strange to the officers who change in a company so frequently. Adding 50 reservists to a company of 100 men will do no harm; adding 85 to a company of 65 will be very different and, if the men added in the second case be untrained recruits, we shall not have a trained unit but a school of instruction.

A great objection to our present strength is the fact that it is so wasteful of money and effort.

IN CONCLUSION

The object of the army is to have a trained force ready for action and to help train the great mass of men that will be called out in case of war. We want as many trained men as possible, both for the ranks and to help prepare others. Since we cannot have a large army we should do all we are able with what we have.

We have in the regular army an expensive plant; the interest on cost and overhead charges form a large part of the annual cost, the cost for privates is relatively small. There is a demand and need for the output, trained soldiers; yet we produce less than half of what we could for the same cost, except pay of privates. With no increase in interest on plant and pay of officers and senior non-commissioned officers and administration, we could more than double our output of trained men and more than double our efficiency for war, and the training would be much better.

A private corporation doing business this way would probably go into bankruptcy.

One thing should be made a fixed policy and made positive law now so that in case of a real war it will be carried out. All organizations received into the service for the war must be at full strength.

New organization in war

We shall require in such a war a very large army which means the utilizing of all the organizations we now have and forming many new ones. By filling all existing organizations to war strength we reduce the number of new ones to be formed and utilize their training capacity to the best advantage; they can not be taken at their existing strength and state of training and have much value in battle. We shall need so many men that must be trained that we must use what means of training we have to its utmost.

By reducing the number of new organizations, more and better officers can be used for their training; there will be more chance of getting the necessary instructors for them. A few of the right kind of men can fit for service a full strength regiment as well as one of half strength and better officers and non-commissioned officers can be found for it, for there will be fewer required and the average can be higher.

Besides the difference in cost, administration, road space on the march, and the tactical handling when massed in great numbers, are of great importance and are much better done with fewer organizations.

Upon the army today rests a great resposibility. With our small numbers and many faults in organization and stations we must be as nearly ready for a great war as possible; not only personally ready but do what we can to make the organization of a great and efficient army, if it ever becomes necessary, a possibility.

The army's responsibility

This means we must study and know our profession thoroughly, give a helping hand to the national guard when and where we can and to any other organization that does something toward the military training of men who may make up this great army if it has to be raised. We must remember that there are many things to be taught a man before he is an efficient soldier; all he learns before he joins a volunteer regiment is that much of a help.

But our chief duty, after personal qualification, is to make the best soldiers possible out of the men under us. This is what we are paid for and this is worth much more to our country than anything else we can do in peace. We should make the best we can of the conditions as they exist at our post, they may not be favorable for getting the best results but that is no reason for our not getting the best possible.

more. The narrow scope of instruction followed in some companies, and the seeking for the easiest way to kill the drill hour by a few, has helped to give this its prominence in our training.

Target practice
Our target practice is open to criticism in some respects. Its importance can not be overestimated and it must not be slighted, but rational methods should be followed. It is necessary to appreciate fully what is required and wanted.

The individual man must be a fairly good marksman for two reasons: so that he can place his shots in a designated locality, and to give him confidence in himself. The better the men can shoot, other things being equal, the more confidence they have in themselves and in each other. For practical results on the battlefield an expert rifleman is of little if any more value than a marksman. Good, fair shooting by every man in the company is what is desired.

On the battlefield much depends on the confirmed habit, this habit-forming can not be done on the target range, but throughout the year's work. Not to exceed two weeks a year should be allowed to any company for known distance practice on the range. If its work during the rest of the year has been properly done, this is sufficient. The rest of the time is needed for other work. But the time put on field firing, where done in the solution of correct tactical problems, cannot well be excessive. The more of this the better. *Target practice*

The law granting extra pay to expert shots, sharpshooters and marksmen is not believed good in its effect; it gives undue importance to range firing. An expert rifleman without other training and discipline is of but little value on the battlefield, while even a second class shot, well trained and disciplined, is infinitely his superior as a soldier. This law should be amended so as to divide the men into two classes: the best men in each company to be rated as 1st class. To be so rated the man must be thoroughly well trained in *all* his duties, of excellent character and 1st classman or better in target shooting. The extra pay for 1st classmen to be so alloted as to cost the government no more than is now paid for higher classifications. Men have drawn this extra pay for qualification as shots who were of but little account as soldiers. *Extra pay*

Rifle firing among young men in civil life

Rifle firing competitions

should be encouraged. It is a necessary *part* of a soldier's training and is that much accomplished toward making efficient soldiers of them if the occasion arises.

Our rifle competitions take too much time and are allowed to interfere too much with regular training. Officers should not be allowed to compete. Their work during this season is with their companies; they should be learning the duties of an officer not that of the private in the ranks. It is undoubted that a man can not make much of a success teaching what he does not know. The officer must know how to shoot well enough to be an instructor, he must know the theory and have the knack of instructing. He does not need to neglect his regular work for weeks at a time several summers to acquire this at competitions.

The best company instructor in rifle firing the author ever saw on a target range was a first sergeant who himself never made better than marksman. The company was very short on sharpshooters and experts but was still shorter on 3d class men. The poorest instructor he ever saw was an officer whose breast on state occasions was covered with big medals for shooting. He had to spare his own eyes so as to make phenomenal scores; the instruction of the new men in the company was of little importance compared with the former.

The proper garrisoning of the army, to avoid so much necessary labor and afford better opportunities for training, has been given great attention by the War Department. May it soon meet with success. But much can be done even under present conditions to help in this matter. This beautiful parking perfectly kept is pretty, but it takes ground needed for other purposes and requires an immense amount of "fatigue" labor. This labor could be reduced: the parks would not be so pretty but military efficiency would be greater. For which does the government spend its money? **Proper garrisoning**

Our companies should be increased in size to 100 men in peace, in war to 150. Our companies are now too small for good training; it requires too many new men to raise them to war strength, and the present strength is wasteful of money and effort. **Strength of the company**

With the companies at a fixed peace strength of 65 it means much of the time still less. There are not enough men to drill in the regular platoon formations. In our extended

Strength of the company order work the captain is reduced to the capacity of a platoon commander and platoon commanders are out of a job. These men do not get practice in the handling of their proper units and it can not fail to diminish their interest and enthusiasm and result in poorer work as well as in incomplete work.

In the case of war we shall need our regular organizations very promptly and as efficient as possible. At the same time these organizations are certain to lose many officers taken for other duties. The addition of much more than one man to each two then in ranks, even if they have been previously trained, is a serious blow to efficiency. The new men must either be untrained or men from a reserve. If from a reserve they are rusty on many points and are apt to be strange to the officers who change in a company so frequently. Adding 50 reservists to a company of 100 men will do no harm; adding 85 to a company of 65 will be very different and, if the men added in the second case be untrained recruits, we shall not have a trained unit but a school of instruction.

A great objection to our present strength is the fact that it is so wasteful of money and effort.

IN CONCLUSION

The object of the army is to have a trained force ready for action and to help train the great mass of men that will be called out in case of war. We want as many trained men as possible, both for the ranks and to help prepare others. Since we cannot have a large army we should do all we are able with what we have. *Strength of the company*

We have in the regular army an expensive plant; the interest on cost and overhead charges form a large part of the annual cost, the cost for privates is relatively small. There is a demand and need for the output, trained soldiers; yet we produce less than half of what we could for the same cost, except pay of privates. With no increase in interest on plant and pay of officers and senior non-commissioned officers and administration, we could more than double our output of trained men and more than double our efficiency for war, and the training would be much better.

A private corporation doing business this way would probably go into bankruptcy.

One thing should be made a fixed policy and made positive law now so that in case of a real war it will be carried out. All organizations received into the service for the war must be at full strength. *New organization in war*

New organization in war

We shall require in such a war a very large army which means the utilizing of all the organizations we now have and forming many new ones. By filling all existing organizations to war strength we reduce the number of new ones to be formed and utilize their training capacity to the best advantage; they can not be taken at their existing strength and state of training and have much value in battle. We shall need so many men that must be trained that we must use what means of training we have to its utmost.

By reducing the number of new organizations, more and better officers can be used for their training; there will be more chance of getting the necessary instructors for them. A few of the right kind of men can fit for service a full strength regiment as well as one of half strength and better officers and non-commissioned officers can be found for it, for there will be fewer required and the average can be higher.

Besides the difference in cost, administration, road space on the march, and the tactical handling when massed in great numbers, are of great importance and are much better done with fewer organizations.

Upon the army today rests a great resposibility. With our small numbers and many faults in organization and stations we must be as nearly ready for a great war as possible; not only personally ready but do what we can to make the organization of a great and efficient army, if it ever becomes necessary, a possibility.

The army's responsibility

This means we must study and know our profession thoroughly, give a helping hand to the national guard when and where we can and to any other organization that does something toward the military training of men who may make up this great army if it has to be raised. We must remember that there are many things to be taught a man before he is an efficient soldier; all he learns before he joins a volunteer regiment is that much of a help.

But our chief duty, after personal qualification, is to make the best soldiers possible out of the men under us. This is what we are paid for and this is worth much more to our country than anything else we can do in peace. We should make the best we can of the conditions as they exist at our post, they may not be favorable for getting the best results but that is no reason for our not getting the best possible.

The army's responsibility

The quitter, the man who does as little as possible, who always wants to be away from troops because things are not as he thinks they should be, or who does nothing because he cannot do it exactly as laid down, is a curse to the army; he should leave the service and sell ribbons.

Rational, systematic training besides producing the greatest military efficiency will keep the men interested in their work and will occupy more of their time; the men will be more contented. Interested and contented men will furnish a smaller sick report and fewer deserters. There will be less dissipation hence less punishment.

Discontent, ennui, a constant grouch, injure digestion and bring on other physical ills. This is another responsibility resting on officers—that for the men under them. With young men we have a great influence on their characters and future careers. We make men better fit for life's work or turn them back worse than we found them.

To the credit of the army it can be said that in most cases an enlistment served therein is a benefit to the majority who so serve. The men are physically and mentally better for a short service and I believe morally.

There is certainly less excessive drinking among our soldiers in nearly all regiments than in a corresponding number of civilians in the same vicinity, and the same is true as to other vices. In personal cleanliness, decency and politeness they are far ahead of the average man of the same social standing as that from which they come. Many employers have recognized this, and are giving preference to discharged soldiers in employment. The uniform makes the man conspicuous and one drunken soldier in a thousand will call for more attention than ten drunken civilians out of five hundred. *The army's responsibility*

The duty of trying to improve the men morally is a military as well as a moral duty. It is in line with what has been said before: the better the man, the more valuable the soldier, the more he can be taught, the more he can help to train others, and the more likely is he to remain in physical condition to be fit for service in the field.

"We have a profession not a trade." Let us take it seriously, appreciate our responsibility, make the best of conditions as we find them, improving them where we can, and train ourselves and those under us to be THE BEST INFANTRY.